Also from the Authors

You can develop the skills to meet the needs of learners in any learning environment.

This approachable, in-depth guide unites the adaptability of Universal Design for Learning with the flexibility of blended learning, equipping educators with the tools they need to create relevant, authentic, and meaningful learning pathways to meet students where they're at, no matter the time and place or their pace and path. With step-by-step guidance and clear strategies, authors Katie Novak and Catlin Tucker empower teachers to implement these frameworks in the classroom, with a focus on cultivating community, building equity, and increasing accessibility for all learners.

As we face increasing uncertainty and frequent disruption to traditional ways of living and learning, *UDL and Blended Learning* offers bold, innovative, inclusive solutions for navigating a range of learning landscapes, from the home to the classroom and all points in between, no matter what obstacles may lie ahead.

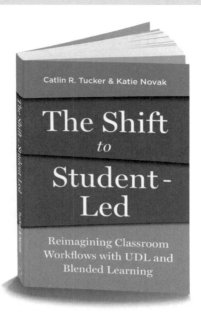

Catlin Tucker and Katie Novak have worked with too many educators who are frustrated and disillusioned with the teaching profession. They know that teachers are drowning in work and unrealistic demands. Many are mentally and emotionally exhausted by the uncertainty and constant change created by the pandemic. In this follow-up to *UDL and Blended Learning*, the authors have set out to help teachers reimagine their approach to this work so that it is sustainable and rewarding.

Each chapter in *The Shift to Student-Led* takes apart one traditional teacher-led workflow, examining the problems it presents teachers and students, what the research says versus what the reality in the classroom is, and how UDL and blended learning can free teachers from the "sage on the stage" role and place students at the center of their learning. These reimagined student-led workflows help students develop self-awareness, internal motivation, and self-regulation skills, which are critical to becoming expert learners.

Intended for K–12 educators, instructional coaches, and school leaders who want to create academically robust, inclusive learning communities, this book is full of principles, strategies, and resources that can be put into practice right away and at any level.

Shift Writing into the Classroom

SHIFT WRITING INTO THE CLASSROOM

WITH UDL AND BLENDED LEARNING

CATLIN R. TUCKER
AND KATIE NOVAK

Shift Writing into the Classroom with UDL and Blended Learning
© 2024 Catlin R. Tucker and Katie Novak

All rights reserved. No part of this publication may be reproduced in any form or by any electronic or mechanical means, including information storage and retrieval systems, without permission in writing by the publisher, except by a reviewer who may quote brief passages in a review. For information regarding permission, contact the publisher at books@impressbooks.org.

> This book is available at special discounts when purchased in quantity for educational purposes or for use as premiums, promotions, or fundraisers. For inquiries and details, contact the publisher at books@impressbooks.org.

Published by IMPress, a division of Dave Burgess Consulting, Inc.
IMPressbooks.org
DaveBurgessConsulting.com
San Diego, CA

Paperback ISBN: 978-1-948334-70-9
Ebook ISBN: 978-1-948334-65-5

Cover design by Sarah Flood-Baumann
Interior design by Liz Schreiter
Edited and produced by Reading List Editorial
ReadingListEditorial.com

For every teacher who enthusiastically embraces their role as lead learner, this book is for you. No matter the subject you teach, we hope the strategies in this book help you to weave writing seamlessly into your classroom. Here's to enhancing your relationships with students and unleashing the inner writer within each one of them.
—*Catlin*

To the all educators who invest in the human side of this work, knowing that the relationships they build with their students are the foundation for meaningful learning experiences. Thank you for all you do!
—*Katie*

Contents

Introduction: The Value of Shifting Writing into Classrooms 1

Chapter 1: UDL and Blended Learning Rerun 16

Chapter 2: Writing across Disciplines (It's Not Just an English Thing) 37

Chapter 3: Blended Instruction to Boot the Sage off the Stage. 56

Chapter 4: Deconstructing and Analyzing Writing Samples. 74

Chapter 5: Pre-writing and Planning 92

Chapter 6: Writing in Class with Teacher Support and Feedback . . 108

Chapter 7: Writing Conferences and Personalized Support 132

Chapter 8: The Power of Peer Feedback. 148

Chapter 9: Self-assessment 163

Chapter 10: Side-by-Side Writing Assessments 185

Conclusion: Humans Are Winning. 203

Notes. 209
Acknowledgments. 215
About the Authors. 218
More from IMPress, Inc.. 220

Tables, Figures, and Planning Templates

Table 1:1: Faculty Meeting Choice Board 21
Table 1.2: Blended Learning Rotation Models 28
Table 2.1: Writing-to-Learn Prompts 43
Table 2.2: Exam Wrapper 45
Table 2.3: Thinking Aloud to Model a Planning and Goal-Setting Strategy 46
Table 2.4: Student-Generated Writing Prompts Using AI Chatbots .. 53
Figure 3.1: Flipped Writing Video Note-Taking Choice Board 65
Table 3.1: Gradual Release Model for Teacher-Led Station 67
Figure 3.2: Writing-Focused Station Rotation Lesson 68
Figure 3.3: No Red Ink Learning Playlist.......................... 70
Table 4.2: Text Structures for Different Genres of Writing 83
Table 4.3: Attributes in Different Genres of Writing 83
Figure 4.1: Student-Designed Rubric Using Success Criteria 86
Figure 4.2: Analyzing Writing Exemplars 87
Table 5.1: Pre-writing Choice Board 101
Table 5.2: STOP and LIST with Student Response 103
Table 5.3. Online Station Choice Board..........................104
Table 5.4. Peer-Feedback Choice Board 105
Figure 6.1: Elementary Opinion Writing Rubric 113
Figure 6.2: Goal-Setting Graphic Organizer 114
Table 6.1: Feedback Session Form 117
Figure 6.3: Writing-Focused Station Rotation 119
Table 6.2: Tips for Running a Teacher-Led Feedback Station for Writing 121
Figure 6.4: DBQ Writing Playlist 124

Table 6.3: Three Feedback Strategies for Teachers Working with Students Online 126

Figure 6.5: Feedback Choice Board 128

Table 7.1: Effective Versus Ineffective Writing Conferences 137

Table 7.2: Writing Conference Example Questions 138

Table 7.3: Writing Conference Form 140

Table 8.1: Rubric to Drive Peer Review 153

Table 8.2: Peer-Feedback Choice Board 154

Table 8.3: Sample Glows and Grows from Peer Review 156

Table 8.4: Memorialize Your Feedback 159

Figure 9.1: Math Self-assessment Rubric: Constructing Viable Arguments 172

Table 9.1: Journal Prompts for Self-assessment 175

Table 9.2: 3-2-1 Writing Self-assessment 176

Figure 10.1: Elementary Narrative Writing Rubric 194

Table 10.1: Blended Learning Models and Strategies 196

Figure 10.2: Document the Names of Students Who Need Follow-up Instruction and Support 198

To access templates and other resources mentioned in this book, use this QR code.

INTRODUCTION

The Value of Shifting Writing into Classrooms

We Need Not Fear ChatGPT

Catlin I remember the morning I woke up to three text messages about ChatGPT. I had no idea what it was or why it inspired three people to text me before 6:30 a.m. I climbed out of bed, turned on my coffee machine, and stood in my dark kitchen doing a Google search. The articles that popped up in the results immediately piqued my interest: "ChatGPT Will End High-School English," "Anti-cheating Education Software Braces for ChatGPT," and "Will ChatGPT Kill the Student Essay?"

It didn't take me long to learn why this new AI technology that specializes in dialogue and can generate sophisticated and original responses to questions in moments was causing such a stir in education. Yet, as I read about it, my response was comparatively calm, even though I'd spent sixteen years teaching high school English. As I set my phone down to consider what I had just read, my initial thought was, *ChatGPT will only kill the student essay and authentic writing if we continue to send inauthentic writing tasks home with students.* If teachers asked students to engage in the writing process in the classroom, be it a lab report, research paper, argumentative essay, or cause-and-effect analysis, they would not need to fear ChatGPT. Technology is not the problem; traditional teaching practices are the problem.

The emergence of this AI technology is another force beyond the classroom that's shining a spotlight on the shortcomings and limitations of the traditional approach to teaching. Two hundred years ago, it made sense for teachers to spend a significant amount of time sharing what they knew with students because they were the sole source of information in the classroom. Now, most students at the secondary level have a powerful computer riding around in their pockets, making information easily accessible. They can do a Google search and access up-to-date information about any topic. Granted, they need a lot of coaching on how to do an effective search, analyze sources for credibility, and think critically about information, but those are skills teachers can help students to cultivate. It's the perfect example of how technology is (or should be) changing the role of teachers and learners. Now that learners have access to limitless information online, why would we spend our precious class time at the front of the room transferring information? Instead, we should be focused on human connection and sitting alongside learners to understand their specific needs and provide individualized instruction and support.

As I think back to my first book with Katie, I remember we felt compelled to write it because COVID had rocked the educational community, pushing educators outside their comfort zones and highlighting the limitations of the one-size-fits-all approach to designing and facilitating learning. We wanted to arm teachers with two complementary frameworks—Universal Design for Learning (UDL) and blended learning—that would allow them to confidently navigate any teaching and learning landscape to ensure all students were progressing toward firm standards-aligned goals and developing into expert learners. With the emergence of AI technology, like ChatGPT, as the latest threat to the status quo, educators can get angry and accuse technology of killing authentic writing and making it easier for students to cheat, or we can get creative and reimagine our approach to this work with a focus on designing for human connection.

> UDL and blended learning are innovative approaches to education that focus on creating inclusive learning environments that meet the diverse needs of all students. Benefits of integrating these frameworks include:
> - more equitable access to grade-level learning
> - increased mastery of learning standards
> - a more self-directed, personalized learning experience
> - the development of twenty-first-century skills, such as critical thinking, problem-solving, collaboration, and communication, which are essential for success in our world
> - more balance for educators as there is a shift to the co-creation of learning experiences, as well as more student autonomy
> - more time and space for authentic, meaningful learning experiences

Move Over, Rosey

Katie   Saturday mornings in the 1980s were made for cartoons. Although the original *Jetsons* episodes were produced in the 60s, the show was syndicated by the time my Saturday morning cartoon ritual began. I was a big fan of Rosey, the family's robotic maid. One of my favorite inventions was the automatic vacuum cleaner that came out of her torso. Growing up, I had a fluffy white Samoyed named Boomer, and vacuuming up his marshmallow-fluff fur seemed like a never-ending task. If only I had a robot to do it for me! Fast-forward a few decades, and many people have indeed welcomed robot vacuums into their homes.

Here's the thing: the robot vacuums of the non-cartoon world don't compare to the real thing. A Roomba can't climb the stairs or get behind furniture. (To be honest, I'm surprised no one has figured that out yet!) Now, before you accuse me of pointing fingers at a vacuum cleaner, hear me out. This kind of technology is meant as a tool and a supplement—something to take an item off our to-do list—but it has limitations. The same is true for chatbots like ChatGPT. Don't believe me? Let's check it out. I decided to go all Jetsons and ask ChatGPT to write this introduction for me. Our dialogue went a little something like this:

> Katie: Can you write an introduction for my book about UDL and blended learning to prove that this tool can't write better than me?
>
> ChatGPT: Sure! Here is a potential introduction for your book about UDL and blended learning:
>
>> Universal Design for Learning (UDL) is a framework for designing educational environments that are inclusive and accessible to all learners. It emphasizes the importance of providing multiple means of representation, expression, and engagement to support the diverse needs and abilities of students. Blended learning, on the other hand, is a teaching approach that combines traditional face-to-face instruction with online learning. By combining the strengths of both modes of instruction, blended learning can create a more flexible and personalized learning experience for students.
>
> Katie: Wow, that is really generic. Cat and I write with much more voice, and we love anecdotes. Can you try again?

ChatGPT: Certainly! Here is a revised introduction that incorporates more voice and storytelling:

> Welcome to our book on Universal Design for Learning (UDL) and blended learning! As educators, we are constantly seeking ways to engage and support all of our students. That's why we were drawn to UDL, a framework that helps us design educational experiences that are inclusive and accessible to all learners. And when it comes to blended learning, we love the flexibility and personalization it offers. By combining face-to-face instruction with online learning, blended learning can provide a tailored education that meets the needs of each student.

Katie: You call this a story? Not cutting it. Please give me a funny anecdote about UDL.

ChatGPT: One time, I was working with a student who struggled with dyslexia. He was having a tough time understanding a history lesson, no matter how I presented the material. I tried using different fonts, colors, and text sizes, but nothing seemed to work. Frustrated and at a loss, I turned to UDL for guidance. I remembered one of the principles of UDL is to provide multiple means of representation, so I decided to try something a little unconventional. I dug out my old theater puppets and used them to act out the lesson, with each puppet representing a different historical figure. It was a bit of a wild idea, but it ended up being a huge success! My student was able to understand the material much better through this hands-on, visual representation, and he even asked if we could do more lessons with the puppets.

Okay, so at this point, you may be thinking, *Wow, that's pretty good.* I would like to add, "For a robot who is not an expert in UDL." Let's examine some problems with the story. First, UDL is about providing options and choices to eliminate barriers. If a student is struggling with dyslexia, inaccessible text may be a barrier that prevents learning about historical figures. A UDL practitioner can help to eliminate that barrier by providing options for students to access digital text, collaborate with classmates to find high-quality multimedia resources, and share what they know using a choice board. A teacher may provide a digital text but certainly wouldn't try every single font size. Rather, the teacher would empower students to customize the display of information, access tools like text-to-speech, and work together to make meaning. Students in classrooms that are universally designed are expert learners and have autonomy in their learning.

What is ironic about ChatGPT's anecdote is that one of my favorite stories is about how I used to think I was universally designing my class because I used puppets to teach *The Old Man and the Sea*. Spoiler alert: this is actually a non-example of UDL. UDL isn't about just making learning fun or bringing puppets to life. Our classrooms are not scenes in *Pinocchio*, for goodness' sake. Instead, UDL invites educators to recognize barriers that prevent students from deep learning and sharing what they know in authentic assessments. Sorry, ChatGPT. I win.

The humble ChatGPT, it turns out, does have its own limitations, which it recognizes as soon as you log in. Here are three it shared with me:

- may occasionally generate incorrect information
- may occasionally produce harmful instructions or biased content
- limited knowledge of world and events after 2021

And the biggest limitation of all is that the robot, for all its capabilities, does not write like I do. And if you know me well, really get to know me, you would know that. It can't come close to my level of sass. Believe me. I tried.

After reading its lackluster and inaccurate portrayal of UDL, I prompted ChatGPT to write like me.

> ChatGPT: I'm sorry, but I am not able to write like you as I do not have enough information about your writing style. Could you provide more context or give me some examples of your writing so that I can better understand your style and try to imitate it?

Being the generous and helpful teacher I am, I shared some of my writing.

> ChatGPT: I apologize if my previous response did not meet your expectations. To write like you, I will try to incorporate the style and tone that you used in the provided text.
>
>> As a teacher at Millfield Elementary School, Karen was always looking for ways to make her classroom more inclusive and accessible for all of her students. She had heard about the concept of Universal Design for Learning, or UDL, and was determined to implement it in her class.
>>
>> One day, Karen decided to try out a UDL approach in her lesson on ancient civilizations. She started by providing multiple ways for students to access the information, including text, audio, and visual resources. She also gave students the option to choose how they wanted to demonstrate their understanding, whether through a traditional essay, a presentation, or a creative project.

> Karen was thrilled to see the results. All of her students were engaged and able to participate in the lesson, and she saw a noticeable improvement in their understanding of the material.

This is what the damn robot came up with. I kid you not. C'mon, ChatGPT, it's like you're not even trying! 😏

So, there is it. Technology can be a useful tool, but as you will learn throughout this book, as we get to know our students, help them to establish their voices, and carve out instructional time for them to write, revise, get feedback, and publish in authentic ways, we will help them realize that the Roomba doesn't hold a candle to the real thing—yet.

It is true that AI technology is advancing rapidly, and we do not know what the bots will be capable of in the future. Regardless, it is important to remember that AI is a tool, and it is up to us, as teachers, to use it in a responsible and ethical manner. As technology becomes more innovative, we should continue to prioritize building relationships with our students and creating a safe and supportive environment for them to develop their unique voices. Additionally, as tempting as it is to leverage technology to provide feedback to students on their writing, we should be intentional about balancing its use with other forms of feedback, such as peer review and teacher-student conferences. The goal of AI-enhanced writing instruction should always be to supplement and enhance traditional teaching methods, not to replace them.

Why We Wrote This Book

AI technology like ChatGPT is one example of a force outside of education threatening the status quo, and it won't be the last. The COVID-19 pandemic, which required teachers to shift quickly to online, hybrid, and concurrent teaching environments, is another example. These disruptions highlight the limitations of traditional education's teacher-led approach. It is not flexible enough to weather the metaphorical storms happening beyond our classroom walls.

Writing is a cognitively challenging task. Students who feel unsure how to complete a piece of writing or who struggle to make sense of concepts and texts may turn to ChatGPT to avoid spending hours struggling through a writing assignment. As long as the bulk of writing is assigned as homework and completed outside of class, there is the potential for students to use technology to find and submit writing that is not their own. In the past, students might have copied and pasted text from various online sources. Teachers concerned about the authenticity of that text could simply google a couple of sentences that seemed suspicious to see if they appeared somewhere online. We have both had the experience of reading a student's writing and immediately questioning if that student wrote the piece we were reading. We can hear our students' voices in our heads as we read their writing, so as soon as the writing felt unfamiliar or did not sound like that student, we would google it. Now, ChatGPT complicates that workflow because it produces original writing that doesn't appear anywhere online.

So, our approach has to change. We want to help teachers in every subject area to reimagine their approach to writing, pulling it into the classroom, where students can write with teacher and peer support. Universally designed blended learning creates the time and space to shift many tasks classically assigned for homework into the classroom where they belong. If educators implement more flexible, universally designed blended learning models, students will have access to inclusive and equitable instruction and support while they write. This eliminates the incentive for students to use a resource like ChatGPT, in which case disruptive technology won't be so scary or threatening.

This book will break down the writing process and demonstrate how teachers can use UDL and blended learning to pull each part of this complex and cognitively challenging process into the classroom. Technology will continue to evolve and become more sophisticated, and so must our approach to teaching and learning. Educators must embrace and invest their time and energy in the aspects of this work that technology cannot do. So, let's be clear about what technology does well and what humans do well.

When teachers transfer information in the classroom, students have one opportunity to "get it." If they lack the vocabulary, background knowledge, focus, or auditory processing needed to take the information in and process it, transferring information in this way is unlikely to yield the intended results. Technology is really good for transferring information. Students can read digital texts, watch videos, listen to podcasts, and explore interactive websites to learn about a topic. When students engage with information online, they have more control over that experience. They can expand text, making it bigger and easier to read. They can pause, rewind, and rewatch a video. They may even be able to adjust the speed of a video to ensure the information is being presented at a pace that works for them. They have the same control over a podcast or audio recording. The ability to control the pace at which they consume and process information presented digitally provides clear advantages over traditional whole-class lectures. So, you might be wondering, why are so many teachers still spending significant time at the front of the room talking when technology can transfer information so effectively?

Human beings are good at watching, listening, empathizing, and responding organically to each other's needs, which, as we've seen from our experiment with ChatGPT, technology cannot do yet. To leverage these unique talents, teachers must architect learning experiences that position students at the center of learning where they can practice, apply, interact, engage, discuss, and collaborate.

The Value of Shifting Writing into Classrooms

That way, we can observe and listen to identify areas of strength and weakness. Then we can adjust the instruction, models, and tasks to challenge students who are ready for more rigorous work and support learners in need of additional instruction or scaffolds.

The goal of this book is to help teachers understand their true value in a classroom and use UDL and blended learning to maximize their impact. Our focus as educators must be on the three C's that bestselling author and research professor Brené Brown writes about: courage, compassion, and connection. Brown's work has shown us that these three C's are essential to building strong, healthy relationships with our students, creating safe and inclusive classroom environments, and ultimately helping our students reach their full potential. By embracing these values and using UDL and blended learning as tools, we can maximize our impact and make a meaningful difference in the lives of our students.

Who This Book Is For

Some people in education hear the word *writing* and assume it is the English teacher's job to help students develop as writers. Incorrect. Writing is a part or should be of every subject area. Writing is a powerful vehicle for capturing thinking, processing information, making powerful connections, reflecting, and sharing learning with an audience. This is true even for our youngest learners. A recent special report in *Education Week* shared the importance of incorporating the science of writing into the science of reading for young learners: "Writing can enhance foundational reading skills and students' knowledge of how words and sentences work. And throughout K–5, students need explicit writing instruction, modeling, tools, and access to rich content so that they can write in increasingly sophisticated ways."[1]

And so this book is for every teacher, from the most seasoned secondary teachers to pre-service teachers preparing to enter the most fabulous profession. Instructional coaches and leaders supporting teachers in shifting practice to embrace UDL and blended learning will also find this book a useful resource. The strategies, resources, and templates will provide structure coaches and administrators can use when working with teachers to design and facilitate lessons that pull the writing process into the classroom.

How This Book Is Organized

Each chapter will tackle a step in the writing process and demonstrate how universally designed blended learning can allow teachers to pull that step into the classroom. Now that you have a better sense of what this book is about and the shifts we advocate for, we invite you to revisit the table of contents at the front of the book. Take a moment to preview the chapter titles, noting which concepts you are most excited to learn about.

The chapters will follow a similar format: First, we start with an engaging anecdote or story, as in previous books. Next, we argue that traditional ways of teaching writing aren't cutting it—and offer evidence that we can increase student writing outcomes if we incorporate more flexible, evidence-based practices. We call this section Research and Reality. Then we offer specific strategies for pulling that step in the writing process into the classroom. These strategies are designed to be flexible enough to work in any teaching and learning landscape—in a classroom, online, or a blend of the two. We will anchor these writing strategies in blended learning and UDL to highlight how universally designed blended learning creates the time and space for students to write in class, where they can access support and feedback.

The Value of Shifting Writing into Classrooms

Next, we offer an AI-enhanced strategy for each workflow. Now, first, we want to say that we totally understand why educators are afraid of chatbots and other futuristic tools disrupting classroom writing instruction. People had the same fears about keyboarding, spell-check, and voice-to-text apps. And look how well those turned out! Let's not be afraid to embrace the tools that make teaching and learning more efficient, freeing up cognitive load for deeper learning experiences. With AI as a tool, we can focus on the parts of writing instruction where we really shine, like building relationships with our students and nurturing their unique voices. So don't be scared of the robots. They're here to help us become even better writing teachers.

Lastly, we offer a wrap-up for each chapter that presents the big takeaways and includes reflection and discussion questions for you, your book study group, or your professional learning community (PLC) to consider and discuss as you read. Finally, we have added an action item to the end of each chapter. This activity is designed to get you acting on what you are learning. It will challenge you to take what you learned and create something you can use with students immediately.

Shifting the writing process into the classroom isn't realistic in a teacher-centered, whole-group, lockstep environment. Writing is a complex, cognitively challenging endeavor that benefits from variable time on task. Some students will move through the process more quickly with less support, while others will need more time and benefit from personalized instruction, peer support, and scaffolds.

Teachers must leverage blended learning models to partner with students and shift them to the center of the writing process if all students are going to progress toward firm, standards-aligned goals. Throughout the book, we make clear connections to the core beliefs at the heart of UDL to ensure that these strategies are accessible, inclusive, and equitable. We describe how moving writing into the classroom can help you to align your practices with the core beliefs:

a) learner variability is the norm, b) all students are capable of working toward firm goals but need flexible means, and c) cultivating expert learners is critical if students are going to engage in the learning process fully. We incorporate ideas from our second book, *The Shift to Student-Led*, into this book, so moving writing into the classroom lightens the teacher's workload, eliminating the need to drag endless stacks of digital or literal papers home to grade in isolation. The universally designed strategies presented in this book position the students as active agents in the writing, editing, reviewing, and revising process, requiring that they think critically about each step of the writing process.

Wrap-Up

We want every teacher reading this book to understand the value of writing across disciplines and feel confident guiding students through the writing process while teaching in a landscape where technologies like ChatGPT make it easier than ever for students to "produce" original writing without much effort. Like our previous book, *The Shift to Student-Led*, we hope to help teachers using UDL and blended learning to find more balance in their lives by reimagining outdated, unsustainable, and often frustratingly ineffective approaches to doing this work so our students can develop more authentic writing voices. Students should not be asked to write in isolation without feedback or support after a long day at school. Similarly, teachers should not have to drag endless piles of paperwork home to provide feedback on or grade. These important teacher responsibilities can and should happen in the classroom, where they can serve as opportunities to connect with learners, strengthen our relationships with them, and meet their individual needs.

The Value of Shifting Writing into Classrooms

Reflect/Discuss

1. Think back to when you first learned about ChatGPT. What were your initial reactions?
2. After reading this chapter, what are you hoping to learn about writing instruction, and how do you think that learning more about student writing will impact your practice?
3. How do you currently teach writing? Take a moment to reflect on how often you assign writing tasks and explicitly teach writing. What is working for you? What is frustrating or challenging about incorporating writing into your content area? Where does the bulk of writing take place? How much time do you currently dedicate to feedback as students write?
4. Set a goal for yourself as you read. What would you like to work toward as an educator? How can you leverage this book to help you make progress toward that goal? How will you reflect on what you are reading and learning (e.g., tweets, discussions, sketchnotes, journaling)?

1

UDL and Blended Learning Rerun

To Rewatch or Wing It, That Is the Question

Katie I love the show *Stranger Things*. In my dreams, I'm as badass as the character Eleven, or El, who has supernatural skills that allow her to access other dimensions, annihilate monsters, and crush soda cans with her mind. Even though I have seen every episode, when a new season comes out, I like to go back and rewatch from the beginning. The sixty-second recap at the beginning of a new season won't cut it. So, before each new season starts, I buckle down for a weekend of Netflix, popcorn, and biokinesis.

Not everyone goes back to the beginning to activate their background knowledge when a new season of a beloved show or sequel to a favorite movie is released—but it is an option, and an option I, for one, appreciate.

Not everyone has this luxury of time or a desire to rewatch previous seasons of a show, but it's an option that some of us find helpful. Imagine if the streaming platform only gave you a brief recap of the previous seasons instead of allowing you to access the full episodes and shared a message like, "Hey, we gave you the opportunity to watch, and you missed it. Sorry." The outrage! It would be frustrating to miss out on important context and character development, and you might not enjoy the new season as much as you could have. The same goes for this book.

Now, in full disclosure, Cat and I cannot open up a gate to another dimension, but like Netflix, we can provide an opportunity to "catch up" on our earlier work if you're not familiar with our previous two collaborations, or if you'd like a recap. Our first collab was *UDL and Blended Learning: Thriving in Flexible Learning Landscapes*. Our "season 2" featured *The Shift to Student-Led: Reimagining Classroom Workflows with UDL and Blended Learning*. If you have read both of those books, and you are familiar with the concepts of Universal Design for Learning (UDL) and blended learning, you may feel ready to move on to chapter 2. If you're new to the concepts or would appreciate a recap, this chapter is for you! To keep it fresh for those of you who have read our previous two books—thank you!—our anecdotes are new, and in each section, we make an explicit connection to writing instruction.

We don't want you to rush into the decision, so we have created a flowchart to help you decide whether to stick around in this chapter or jump ahead to the next one.

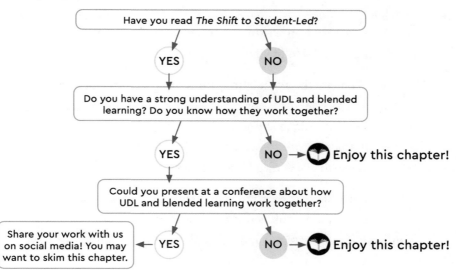

The Power of Universal Design for Learning

As individuals, humans are incredibly dynamic, and one-size-fits-all experiences don't often meet our needs. As you're reading this, you may be thinking, *Yeah, yeah, I get what you're saying, but sometimes in life, you don't get to choose. I mean, no one gives me a choice about whether to file my taxes.* Although, technically, you have many choices when filing your taxes. Bear with us.

UDL practitioners talk about "firm goals, flexible means" as a way of recognizing shared outcomes and the numerous paths that can be used to get to them. When it comes to filing taxes, some people will print out tax forms and mail them. Others will e-file, use a tax preparation software, like TurboTax, or hire an accountant.

When you design learning experiences with UDL, ask yourself: What is it that all learners need to know or be able to do? From there, consider, based on variability, what options and choices you could offer to help them get there. Approaching planning through the lens of UDL requires us to design an environment where students can choose their pathway, product, and pace as they work toward firm goals.

When focused on writing instruction, we as practitioners have to ask ourselves the following questions:

- What are the expectations for writing in my class informally and formally?
- What is unique about writing in my subject area?
- If students are to be successful with writing in my subject area, what specifically do they have to know and do?

We recognize writing as a non-negotiable skill in all subject areas, but there are numerous ways to learn about disciplinary literacy, plan and revise writing, and present writing in authentic ways.

Furthermore, there are numerous scaffolds and materials that students can access as they draft, revise, and publish their writing.

In more traditional models, teachers make all these decisions for students—drafting the writing prompts, creating the rubrics, providing the feedback, and determining how students will share writing. Instead, we need to encourage students to become expert learners, which means they reflect on firm goals for writing and then consider their strengths, interests, mood, areas of need, etc. When we provide opportunities for learners to be more self-aware, they learn to examine multiple pathways and choose the ones that best meet their needs as they work toward firm goals. Allowing students to choose what they need to produce high-quality writing incorporates UDL, social-emotional learning, and trauma-informed and culturally sustaining practices. When we share expectations that students drive their learning experience, we help them become expert learners who are self-aware, recognize the purpose of learning, and can make responsible, strategic decisions about their education.

To universally design lessons, teachers must design instruction with the three UDL principles: multiple means of engagement, multiple means of representation, and multiple means of action and expression.

When teachers provide multiple means of engagement, they are clear about firm goals and provide students with flexible means. Engagement extends beyond recruiting interest and providing choice. We also have to ensure that students can commit to the learning process and continue to put in effort and persistence when they find learning to be challenging, when they would rather be doing something else, or when they aren't interested in the firm goals.

We must create classrooms where students feel safe enough to take risks and know they have options to cope. Creating practices and procedures that embrace frequent breaks, embedded scaffolds, and revisions can optimize student motivation. Since we are asking students to personalize their learning, it is important that we offer frequent opportunities for them to get feedback from peers and adults, reflect on their decisions, and course-correct if necessary.

Representation is the process of curating and presenting information to learners. Over the last two hundred years of education, the primary means of representation have been text and talking (i.e., the whole-class lecture). Text is a problem for some people. Obviously, if you have a visual impairment, then printed text creates a significant barrier. But it is also a problem for those who are English language learners or struggle with decoding, reading comprehension, or have dyslexia. Talking or lecturing can also be a problem, as it requires students to be hearing and have strong auditory processing. Additionally, lecturing is often a passive activity that fails to engage the learner.

As the founders of UDL state in *Universal Design for Learning: Theory and Practice*, "No single medium works for every learner, nor does it for every subject. . . . To promote understanding of information, concepts, relationships, and ideas, it is critical to provide multiple ways for learners to approach them." When teachers provide multiple means of representation, learners get to make choices about how they learn, build knowledge, and explore resources as they work toward firm goals.

Imagine you attend a faculty meeting where the goal is that all educators will share best practices in writing across the curriculum. To activate background knowledge, there are printed copies of a peer-reviewed article on the evidence base of writing and learning. The task is simple. You will have twenty minutes to read the article in silence, and then you will join small groups to make connections between the article and your own practice. What fun!

Both of us have experienced meetings like this. Here's the thing: we are 100 percent certain that a single article will not meet the needs of all educators.

Imagine, instead, that administrators have created a choice board with multiple means of representation that models UDL and exemplifies blended learning. Before the meeting, you receive an email about the purpose of your time together and are given access to a digital choice board, like the one in Table 1.1. This would eliminate the need for teachers to scramble for highlighters and reading glasses while providing the option to print out articles for those who prefer to read a hard copy. How else would this change the dynamics of the meeting?

Table 1:1: Faculty Meeting Choice Board

Read Something	Listen to Something
Choose one or more of the following articles to prepare for the discussion about writing in your content area. Read it alone or find some colleagues and read it aloud together.	Choose one of the following podcasts about writing in all content areas. You can put on your walking shoes and earbuds and listen while getting some steps in!
Watch Something	Put It in Action
Pop some popcorn and have a viewing party where you view videos of teachers discussing how they integrate writing into every class. These videos will help you learn more to prepare for the discussion.	Choose one of the following learning-to-write activities and put it into action. You can work alone or find a buddy! You can share your experiences in the discussion.

Lastly, UDL calls for teachers to provide multiple means of action and expression, so learners have opportunities to share their progress as they work toward firm goals. Students often have to share their learning in a one-size-fits-all way when it comes to writing. For example, standards require all students to produce clear and coherent writing in which the development, organization, and style are appropriate to the task, purpose, and audience.

When we unpack this standard through the lens of our respective content areas, we can determine acceptable evidence and then honor our students and allow them to choose the best way to learn about task, purpose, and audience, develop and organize their writing, and hone their voice and style.

It may seem that some standards do not allow for this level of flexibility, but we are confident there is always a way to shift autonomy and decision-making to the learner. If the firm goal is to write informational text, for example, then all students will, in fact, produce writing. Students can choose to handwrite, type, or use voice-to-text. They may have the option to work with peers or use tools like graphic organizers and sentence stems.

The power of UDL lies in recognizing variability, articulating firm goals, and shifting decision-making to students to foster expert learning. This release of responsibility is most effective when teachers plan instruction using UDL in a blended learning model.

Family Dinners and Training Tiny Humans

Catlin When I was growing up, my mom was an attorney who worked long hours, but she somehow made the time to whip up elaborate meals each evening for dinner. She'd turn on Van Morrison, Tom Petty, or the Beatles and hum to the music while she moved around the kitchen chopping, stirring, and sautéing. I remember the smells of garlic and onions wafting down the hall and into my room as I labored over my homework, and I would hop up when my mom called, "Dinner is ready!"

I have vivid memories of eating her chicken and dumplings or vegetable curry while listening to "Brown Eyed Girl," "Runnin' Down a Dream," or "Can't Buy Me Love" and taking turns sharing stories about our day. It didn't matter how bad my day at school had been. I might have had a falling-out with a friend, played terribly in a soccer scrimmage, or bombed a test, but these moments at the dinner table erased all that. We connected and commiserated and laughed. It was often the highlight of my day.

When I had children of my own, I wanted to instill the same values about the importance of eating together and engaging in conversation about the day. As a fairly new mother, I had no idea that it takes *years* of practice, reviewing expectations, and reinforcing norms to get to a place where a family dinner with tiny humans is actually enjoyable. Family dinners are not for the faint of heart! You have to believe in their value and be committed to them.

Both of my children tested my commitment to family dinners in different ways. My daughter, Cheyenne, was a fabulous eater. I would organize food items on her plate—a scoop of pasta, tiny pieces of cut-up chicken, and vegetables. She ate everything and rarely showed any preference for one food over another. The eating part of dinner was easy street with her. It was the talking that was a challenge. She is the most verbal child I have ever met! So, we had to work on taking turns and listening to other people. I had to repeatedly remind her to breathe, chew, and listen, namely to her brother, when others were talking. She would get frustrated with us because she had so much she wanted to say and did not like having to take turns talking. Our dinners were a training ground for the early development of her listening skills. It was an arduous process, teaching her how to be a considerate member of the conversation.

By contrast, my son is a great listener when anyone else is talking. It was eating that presented the challenges for him at the dinner table. He loves carbohydrates—pasta, bread, and rice. Name a carbohydrate, and he's a fan. I had gotten so used to preparing my daughter's plate with a little bit of everything that it took a minute for me to realize that Maddox would eat up the pasta, ask for more, and never get around to his broccoli or green beans. I would get so frustrated with him for skipping his veggies and loading up on pasta, but I quickly realized I could not approach dinners with him like I approached them with my daughter. I had to adapt to this new member of our dining party!

Instead of putting everything on his plate at the start of the meal, I only put the vegetables on his plate. The first time I did this, he scanned the rest of our plates and lurched in my direction in an attempt to grab pasta off my dish. I nipped that right in the bud! I calmly explained that he could have pasta after eating his vegetables. He did not like that. He whined and complained until he realized I was not budging. Then, with great annoyance and an impressive amount of side-eye for a toddler, he ate his veggies and pushed his plate in my direction with a grunt. I smiled, thanked him for his cooperation, and added pasta to his plate.

From that day on, he always got his veggies first. Sometimes he would look warily at the vegetable and ask me, "What's next?" Translation: he wanted to know if what he would get afterward was worth powering through the squash or brussels sprouts or other vegetable he wasn't wild about. Eventually, he got used to eating the vegetables and then getting the main course, but it took a lot of training, patience, and working through frustration. There were a couple of nights when he left the table having eaten next to nothing, and by the time we were done with books and bath time, he had reevaluated, reluctantly climbing back into his seat to eat cold vegetables while I reheated the rest of the meal.

Now as I sit and enjoy a nice meal and conversation with my two teenagers, I am so grateful I did not give up on family dinners. I only wish someone had warned me about how challenging it would be and could have reminded me to give myself some grace on the evenings when dinner was an absolute disaster! In those moments when I felt like I was failing or questioned if I would ever enjoy dinner as a family, I wish I had known it was all part of the process. Now I know that the most rewarding moments in life are hard-earned, take time, and require repeat practice and a lot of dedication. My kids needed almost thirteen years of nightly dinners to develop the skills required to eat a healthy meal and engage in an equitable conversation. Now, I feel confident that when they visit a friend's home or go out to dinner, they'll have the skills they need to navigate those moments successfully.

The Power of Blended Learning

Just as enjoyable family dinners didn't happen overnight, the shift to student-centered learning using blended learning models is a journey that takes time. Because blended learning is a fundamental shift in control over the learning experience from teacher to student, we must train our students to become self-directed learners. Students need clear expectations, consistent routines, support and scaffolds, feedback, and practice to develop these skills. Just as Cat wanted to prepare her children to go out into the world with the skills required to be considerate dining companions, we want to prepare our students with the skills necessary to direct their learning, regulate their behavior, and make responsible decisions.

Much like the dream of fun family dinners, the shift to blended learning requires commitment, patience, and the conviction that learning should strive to place students at the center of the learning experience. It won't happen overnight, but when it does happen, it is magical and well worth the time and energy required to make it happen!

Let's start with a clear definition since the phrase "blended learning" has been thrown around a lot in the last few years, but it isn't always anchored in a clear definition. Blended learning is the combination of active, engaged learning online with active, engaged learning offline to give students more control over the time, place, pace, and path of their learning experience.

We believe the most important part of this definition is "active, engaged learning." Ultimately, achieving the goal of blended learning to shift students to the center of the learning process demands by definition that they play an active role in that process. They must be the ones thinking, doing, discussing, collaborating, problem-solving, creating, and reflecting. We recognize this is a much more cognitively and socially demanding role for students who may be very comfortable passively consuming information and observing their teachers doing the work in a lesson. The truth is that it is much easier to be a student in a teacher-centered classroom and much more challenging to be a student in a student-centered classroom. Yet the skills and habits students hone when they are doing the work and driving their learning experiences in directions that are meaningful, interesting, and relevant to them will serve them long after they leave our classrooms—just as my children will be able to take what they learned at our dinner table into their lives as adults.

There are many different ways to combine this active, engaged learning online and offline, which is why there are a variety of blended learning models and strategies, as pictured in Table 1.2.

The taxonomy of blended learning models is evolving as educators experiment with different ways of combining online and offline learning. For example, choice boards can be composed entirely of offline activities, which would not fall under the umbrella of blended learning. By contrast, a teacher can create a choice board with a mix of online and offline learning activities that position the student as an active agent. We provided an example of this type of choice board, the faculty meeting choice board in Table 1.1. In this case, choice boards are absolutely a blended learning strategy. Similarly, the 5Es instructional model—engage, explore, explain, elaborate, and evaluate—initially designed to encourage student-led inquiry in science classrooms can also be used to combine active, engaged learning online and offline, making it a robust blended learning model appropriate for any subject area or grade level.

Not only do these blended learning models work well in a physical classroom, but they also work well for entirely online classes or in a blend of the two. We've long known blended learning could work in classrooms using the rotation models highlighted in Table 1.2. However, we were thrilled by how well these models worked when students were learning remotely from home during the pandemic.

Even the station rotation model, which many educators assume must take place in a classroom where they can arrange physical stations, works beautifully online. During the pandemic, educators used the station rotation model by breaking a class into smaller groups and giving each group time to log onto a video conference. Teachers used the main room to work with a small group at their "teacher-led station," differentiating instruction, leading interactive modeling sessions, facilitating small-group discussions, and providing feedback on student work. Depending on the nature of the online station, students worked asynchronously through an activity or joined a collaborative breakout room to work with their peers on a shared task. The offline station allowed students to log off the video call, take a break from the screen, and engage with a tactile or experiential task. For example, students might go outside and make observations, perform fieldwork to gather data, interview a family member, complete pencil-and-paper practice, or create a concept map. The possibilities were limitless!

The flexibility of these blended learning models is exciting because it means teachers do not need one skill set to design and facilitate learning in a classroom and another skill set to work with students online. Instead, teachers who develop confidence using blended learning models to design accessible, inclusive, and equitable learning experiences can confidently traverse any teaching and learning landscape.

Table 1.2: Blended Learning Rotation Models

Blended Learning Models and Strategies

The Whole-Group Rotation Model

The entire class rotates between online and offline learning activities that attempt to balance the online with the offline and the individual with the collaborative to maximize the power and potential of the learning community while leveraging technology to create personalized pathways. While students are working online, the teacher is free to work with individuals or small groups of learners who need more instruction, modeling, guided practice, feedback, or support.

Example:

- Teachers can begin class with offline retrieval practice to help students revisit previous concepts or skills or anticipate new ones.
- Then they can transition the class online and give students the option to explore information presented in a text or video, depending on their preference.
- Once students have had the opportunity to self-pace through that information, the teacher can provide additional instruction or guide an interactive modeling session.
- After the direct instruction and modeling, the teacher can allow students to decide whether to practice and apply learning online with a computer program or offline with a partner.

The Station Rotation Model

Small groups of students rotate through a series of stations or learning activities that combine offline and online learning. Typically, a station rotation includes a teacher-led station, online stations, and offline stations. This model frees the teacher to work with small groups of learners to more effectively differentiate instruction, models, supports, and scaffolds for learners with different needs, abilities, language proficiencies, learning preferences, and interests.

Example:
- The teacher-led station can be focused on onboarding students to a particular strategy or skill using an "I do–We do–Groups do–You do" progression and differentiating the experience for each group.
- The online station can engage students in an asynchronous discussion designed to get them accessing and sharing their prior knowledge on a topic.
- The offline station can ask students to read a text and work with a partner to create a concept map or sketchnote.

Flipped Classroom

Teachers use video strategically to shift instruction online, where students can self-pace through explanations, pausing, rewinding, and rewatching as needed. Students can manipulate the video instruction by slowing down the video or adding captions to increase accessibility. Teachers can spend more time supporting students as they take what they've learned and attempt to apply it.

Example:
- Prior to the video, teachers may want to pre-teach vocabulary to remove any barriers to accessing the information in the video or present a "hook activity" to pique student interest in the topic.
- Teachers can record a mini-lesson explaining a concept (e.g., kinetic energy) using a mix of text and visuals. They can wrap the video in an Edpuzzle lesson that prompts students to answer specific questions about the content of the video or pair the video with a guided note template.
- After students have seen the video, teachers can strategically pair or group students for a follow-up activity that challenges them to apply what they learned in the video.

Playlist/Individual Rotation

A playlist is a series of learning activities presented in a sequence, moving learners toward a desired outcome or learning objective. Playlists have on-demand instruction and models, combine online and offline learning activities, provide meaningful choices, and—ideally—provide teachers with opportunities to conference with students as they progress through the playlist.

During these conferences, teachers can review formative assessment data, discuss student progress, and modify individual playlists. Playlists can be differentiated for groups of learners at different levels of readiness and can be personalized via teacher check-ins throughout the process.

Example:

- Teachers can create a sequence of learning activities to guide students through the process of learning about fractions, writing an essay, or completing a multi-step performance task.

Choice Boards

Choice boards can be organized to provide students with a mix of online and offline activities that target specific standards, skills, processes, vocabulary, etc.
The goal is to allow students to choose the specific activities they think they will enjoy and benefit from spending time on. As students self-pace through items on a choice board, the teacher is freed to work with individual students or small groups. They can use the time created by a choice board to conference with students or conduct side-by-side assessments of completed work.

> **Example:**
> - Teachers may create a choice board designed to support review and practice, targeting specific skills, concepts, and vocabulary. Alternatively, they can create a standards-aligned board to provide students with meaningful choices about how they engage with a particular standard or skill.

UDL and Blended Learning: A New Dimension

Back in the world of *Stranger Things*, when Eleven unlocks new and scary dimensions, terrible monsters are unleashed and take over the world. Not good. But when you use the power of UDL and blended learning to unlock student-led learning in your classroom, the only monster you'll be confronting is the three-headed one of having to teach, plan, and assess all student writing by yourself. Slay it, win back your time, and embrace this new dimension!

UDL makes it crystal clear that learners are wonderfully diverse and that a diversity of experience, skills, interests, and preferences strengthens a learning community, leading to a richer and more dynamic learning experience. That diversity also demands that we—as architects of learning experiences—strive to make writing accessible, inclusive, and equitable by prioritizing flexible pathways and meaningful choices. Teachers fundamentally understand the value of the beliefs at the core of UDL, but they may not be sure how to actualize these beliefs and put them into practice in ways that are sustainable. Blended learning provides concrete structures teachers can use to design learning experiences that shift control to learners.

Blended learning can free the teacher from the role of "expert at the front of the room." Instead of simply transferring information, teachers can use blended learning to become more effective facilitators, working directly with students to support their individual writing progress. By leveraging digital tools and resources, teachers can provide students with personalized feedback and support, while also freeing up time for more meaningful interactions and relationship building. This shift in teaching practices can lead to more sustainable, long-term growth for both teachers and students. Blended learning without a firm grounding in UDL principles can result in superficial technology use and lackluster learning experiences. UDL without blended learning can make designing flexible pathways feel overwhelming and unsustainable. Let's examine some of the synergies between UDL and blended learning.

Learner Variability, Flexible Pathways, and Expert Learning

We've established that learners are different and will not all travel from point A to point B effectively along the same path. Universally designed blended learning prioritizes student agency as a vehicle to honor this variability and allow students to choose the best path as they engage in writing-to-learn and learning-to-write activities (more on this in the next chapter). For example, students will vary in their preferences when it comes to planning their writing. If the goal is to have students plan a strategy for a written product, some will prefer to make an outline, others will create graphic organizers, and still others may enjoy viewing exemplars to build background knowledge and clarify expectations. The more choices a learner has in a given learning experience, the less likely they are to encounter barriers that stall their progress or result in writer's block!

But offering these choices may feel overwhelming in the context of a teacher-led whole-group lesson. Instead, using blended learning models, like the playlist model, or strategies, like a choice board, allows for more student control over the time, pace, and path of their experience. This makes offering options more manageable. For example, a teacher can create a writing playlist to help students prepare for writing. The playlist may present information in a variety of formats—text, video, interactive websites—and allow students to examine the writing prompt, rubrics, exemplars, and tools to help them plan. It can include activities, like analyzing and discussing the writing prompt, and invite students to decide whether they'd like to discuss with a partner or post their ideas to an online discussion board as they summarize success criteria. The goal of the playlist is to shift control over the pace of their progress to the learner while providing them with various pathways through the material.

UDL is grounded in the belief that all students can and should become expert learners. Because blended learning requires that learners take an active role in the learning process, it is important for them to be resourceful, strategic, motivated, and self-aware. Together UDL and blended learning can help students develop the characteristics of expert learners because learning is a shared endeavor, or partnership, between the teacher and the learners. The more teachers release responsibility to learners (over time and with lots of scaffolding), the more opportunities students have to understand themselves as writers and to select strategies and pathways that will help them succeed in developing their voices. Through metacognitive skill building, conferencing with teachers, seeking feedback from peers, and engaging in regular reflection, students can develop the skills and attributes needed to be expert writers, allowing them to thrive in our classrooms and beyond.

Workflows That Actually Work

Ultimately, we believe that the traditional workflows in education don't actually work for anyone. They create mountains of paperwork that teachers feel compelled to grade, which robs them of the time and energy they need to design dynamic student-centered learning experiences. These ineffective workflows steal precious time in class when teachers should work alongside individuals and small groups of learners, supporting their progress. And they cheat students out of the opportunity to take active roles in the learning process, drive their learning in directions that feel interesting and relevant, and become expert learners.

The goal of this book is to reimagine components of writing instruction that are not working. We will weave together the beliefs at the core of UDL and the principles guiding the implementation of UDL with blended learning models to help teachers shift students to the center of every learning experience. Instead of asking, "How can I _____?" we want you to ask, "How can my students _____?" This simple shift can help us to establish new practices that are more sustainable and that lighten the teacher's load while actively engaging students in every part of the writing process.

Wrap-Up

Traditional approaches to writing instruction overburden teachers and prevent students from building autonomy and agency in their writing. What was previously unimaginable becomes possible when we leverage best practices, use innovative technology solutions, and co-create learning experiences with students.

When we transfer the power of design, decision-making, and collaboration to the learners we serve, we create spaces that allow them to build the skills necessary for success. Just as importantly, we create a more balanced workload for ourselves, as we aren't doing work for students that they are capable of doing themselves.

Reflect/Discuss

1. We know classrooms have a wide spectrum of needs, abilities, preferences, and interests. Why do you think so many

teachers still design whole-group writing prompts where students are expected to plan, draft, and publish their writing in one-size-fits-all ways? What makes it challenging for teachers to honor learner variability in the design of their writing lessons?
2. If expert writers are motivated, resourceful, strategic, and self-aware, what changes need to happen in classrooms to help students develop these attributes?
3. Which blended learning models have you used in your work with students? How might you use these models to create more time and space for writing in the classroom?
4. What synergies do you see between UDL and blended learning? How do you see them working together to create more accessible, inclusive, and equitable learning experiences as students design writing that is focused on task, purpose, and audience?

Putting It into Practice

As we embark on this journey to explore new, more sustainable practices focused on writing instruction across the curriculum, think about your current approach to teaching and assessing writing and identify a part of the process that isn't working well. Describe that workflow in writing using a formalized writing process, like an essay or letter to your department, or something more informal like a series of social media posts or a blog. Some questions to consider:

- What are you currently doing to teach and assess writing?
- What parts of it are working? Which are not, and why aren't they?
- How is writing instruction creating an imbalance in your teaching life?
- Once you've identified an unsustainable practice or something that isn't working for students, ask, "How can my

students _____?" and reimagine this workflow, positioning the students to do the work.

Once you have reimagined what writing instruction could look like in your content area, share the idea with your colleagues or personal learning network (PLN) for feedback.

2

Writing across Disciplines (It's Not Just an English Thing)

For the Love of a Skillet Brownie

Katie For every holiday and birthday, my husband insists that our kids forego the traditional Hallmark card and forces them to design their own greeting cards. This year, on my birthday, my seven-year-old son knocked it out of the park. He wrote, "Mom. I love you so much, but not in that way. You are the smartest person I have ever seen love you. You are so fun can we go to 99's restaurant. Write the date we can go!!!" The pièce de résistance was that a quarter of the card provided space for my response with a giant arrow and a pen taped to the corner.

I loved everything about the message, especially the "I love you so much, but not in that way." (I inquired what "in that way" meant to a seven-year-old, and his response was, "I don't want to marry you." Okay then.) He didn't write the canned "I love you, Mom, you're so awesome" card. He knew exactly what he was doing. He had a purpose, he knew his audience, and he shot his shot. His writing, you see, was both narrative and argumentative, as the (not so) subtle subtext in his request was that I honor his love with a bowl of free popcorn and a skillet brownie at his favorite restaurant.

So, did we go to the 99? You bet we did! We sat at a high-top, our fingers greasy with buttered popcorn, and watched the Celtics game. And that is the power of authentic writing. How can we harness the motivation of a seven-year-old to write for a specific task and purpose in our classrooms? How can we design writing prompts so our students set personal goals, create plans, and put Hallmark cards to shame? We have to better understand what it means to write across the curriculum.

Out of sheer morbid curiosity, I asked ChatGPT to share the research base on Writing Across the Curriculum (WAC), hoping I would be disappointed with the results. It spit out a generic response that included, "A study published in the *Journal of Research in Science Teaching* found that students who participated in a WAC program in a science class showed significant improvements in their writing skills and their understanding of scientific concepts compared to students who did not participate in the program."

Welp, that is not helpful AT ALL if I can't read the original research study or cite it. I asked, "What is the citation for that research?" Do you know what I got? This brilliant and beautiful response.

> ChatGPT: I apologize, but I am unable to provide a citation for the research I mentioned as I am not able to browse the web and do not have access to specific sources.

Oh, ChatGPT, do not apologize. I appreciate your vulnerability, and I'm over the moon that you're staying in your lane. Luckily, I can use my brain, my research skills, and my passion for all things data-nerd to share the research and reality of writing across the curriculum. And, of course, Cat and I can interweave our own analogies and stories to make the research come alive through the lenses of UDL and blended learning. So, if you want to know what WAC is, you can hit up Artificial Intelligence. If you want to know how to bring it to life in your learning environment with concrete, practical strategies, keep on reading.

Research and Reality

The third edition of *UDL Now!* notes that one possible criticism of UDL is that it focuses too much on engaging students and not enough on academic rigor and learning.[1] This could not be further from the truth. UDL is a proactive and rigorous curriculum-design process that begins with identifying firm goals. All teachers have goals and standards for their learners. To be successful, students need to master those goals. To ensure that students have equitable opportunities to do this, teachers need to design the curriculum with those firm goals in mind.

We argue that every classroom should have firm goals for student writing every day, while recognizing that many students will face barriers when we assign writing if we do not scaffold the writing process. When writing, students must engage in a multi-step process of goal-setting, planning, drafting, evaluating, revising, and editing. Dr. Gary Troia, associate professor of special education at Michigan State University, where he is also a principal investigator with the Literacy Achievement Research Center, recommends that writing be taught in all subject areas: "The belief is that writing affords students extended opportunities to think about, manipulate, and transform ideas and reflect on their existing knowledge, beliefs, and confusions."[2]

The challenges students face should not lower expectations for their writing. Rather, educators must recognize the barriers that prevent them from producing high-quality writing and scaffold instruction to address those barriers in all content areas. When students have to master a specific skill like writing, there are UDL guidelines that encourage teachers to provide options for students to set goals, activate their background knowledge, offer models and rubrics, and supply mastery-oriented feedback. Together, these practices provide invaluable scaffolding for students as they write across the curriculum.

Writing Across the Curriculum (WAC) is a movement designed to ensure that students have frequent and significant opportunities to write, revise, and discuss their writing in each of their classes. It is often attributed to Susan H. McLeod, a research professor and writing program distinguished scholar at the University of California, Santa Barbara, but although WAC started at colleges and universities, many PK–12 school districts have WAC initiatives.

The WAC model recognizes that writing and thinking are closely aligned, and therefore, writing belongs in the entire curriculum.[3] When writing is seen as the responsibility of English teachers alone, too often, students will only have extended opportunities to write and revise in their humanities coursework.

Research is clear that writing increases achievement outcomes as the development of students' writing skills improves their capacity to learn.[4] This is true of elementary, middle, and high school students.[5] WAC models require students to identify a clear purpose, topic, text production method, audience, and type of writing to accomplish a specific task.[6] How often do we provide opportunities for students to do that across the content areas? Instead, we tend to rush over this stage, simply providing a prompt and telling our students their task, their purpose, and their audience, which leads them to rote answers, generic responses, and no ownership of or investment in the writing process.

WAC is often broken down into writing-to-learn activities and disciplinary literacy. Writing to learn is when students write for themselves as the audience across the content areas. This encourages low-stakes/ungraded writing activities and assignments to promote exploratory, retrospective, and reflective learning through activities like learning journals, reflections, and online discussions.[7] Empirical studies that examine the impact of writing-to-learn strategies did not indicate any notable differences in the effectiveness of these strategies across content areas and grade levels, so they can be implemented in every classroom.[8]

Disciplinary literacy, sometimes referred to as discourse communities, emphasizes more formal assignments, teaching writing as a way to communicate authentically within each discipline.[9] The International Literacy Association published a leadership brief, "Content Area and Disciplinary Literacy Strategies and Frameworks," which notes the importance of composing and revising texts in all subject areas: "Across disciplines, students can brainstorm and organize initial ideas in visual, graphical, or written formats; they can read their work aloud to help them determine whether it makes sense and flows; and they can improve drafts through revising and editing after receiving specific feedback from their peers and their teachers."[10] These strategies can be planned and shared among interdisciplinary teams.

Other aspects of disciplinary literacy are unique to each content area. As an example, a well-thought-out metaphor may enhance a piece of writing in an English class but would not be appropriate for a written deconstruction of a math problem or the concise, factual writing needed in science.[11] Recognizing the needs of each discipline connects back to the value of WAC, which is understanding task, purpose, and audience. Both of us love a good story, and throughout this book, we go off the rails with memories and analogies. This is intentional, as the audience of this book is educators, and we are known for our practical, informational writing style. That being said, we promise you that our doctoral dissertations were starkly different. We recognized and honored the scholarly nature of the dissertation process, and we changed the style of our writing as a result. Students need to know the rules of writing in each discipline in order to be prepared to write like scientists, mathematicians, historians, and literary authors.

Both informal and creative writing through writing-to-learn activities and formal writing through disciplinary literacy provide opportunities for students to reflect, think critically, and learn at higher levels. In the next section, we offer concrete strategies to make these practices a part of your classroom routines by implementing UDL and blended learning.

Strategy #1: Assign Daily Writing-to-Learn Activities

We are both fans of analogies, and we love one shared by Joan Sedita, the founder of the professional learning organization Keys to Literacy.

> Subject-area teachers sometimes feel overwhelmed with all of the content they must cover during a school year, and it is understandable if at some point you feel there is not enough time to teach writing. Using a plate of food as a metaphor, content teachers may view writing instruction as one more thing to add to an already crowded plate. However, content teachers need to recognize that teaching students how to write about what they are learning gives the students a strong foundation upon which they can access and add more content. When students have strong literacy skills, they have a solid plate to hold all of the content that must be learned.

You can leverage multiple blended learning models to integrate writing-to-learn activities to create a solid plate for learning. One example of an ongoing writing-to-learn activity is a learning journal. Using the principles of UDL, you can provide students with numerous options and choices for how to keep their journals. For example, you may want to provide a template for a digital journal using a document or a slide deck, while some students may prefer more traditional writing using a notebook or a sparkly journal.

As students learn in your content area, you can prompt them to reflect in writing using their journals, combining words and visuals. Because this is low-stakes and not graded, it does not shift additional responsibilities onto you as a teacher. You can incorporate learning journals into existing practices by requiring students to use the journal for do-now activities, entry prompts, and exit tickets. For example, you can integrate an activity in a learning playlist where students explore resources and then share what they've learned by choosing one content question and one interpretative question to respond to in writing (Table 2.1; via the WAC Clearinghouse[12]).

Table 2.1: Writing-to-Learn Prompts

Content Questions	Interpretative Questions
• What was the most important idea in the lesson? What other ideas were important in this lesson? • What particularly striking example do you recall from the lesson? • Which idea that we talked about today most interested you and why? • If you had to restate the concept in your own terms, how would you do that? • If you had to compare this idea to something else to create an analogy, what would you compare it to and why?	• What connections can you make between X and Y? • How does today's discussion build on yesterday's? • How did you connect with this lesson personally? • How does this lesson change your thinking on the idea? • How could you write about your new insight? • How does this reading/writing/ discussion/group work build on our earlier discussion of the larger concept of X?

Another common writing-to-learn activity at the college level is an exam wrapper (Table 2.2). An exam wrapper is a low-stakes writing assignment that students complete before taking an assessment and again after they receive feedback on the assessment as a means to get them thinking and writing about their study skills and learning. The questions "wrap" around the assessment to build more metacognitive reflection about learning. In *The Shift to Student-Led*, we share prompts for before and after an assessment. Consider using these questions or adapting them in an exam wrapper journal so students can reflect on the patterns of their assessment preparation throughout your course.

In addition to using the wrapper concept for assessment, you can use it as a pre- and post-reflection to get students thinking more deeply about any learning activity. For example, before a small-group discussion or an active reading activity, you can ask students to spend time reflecting on their strengths, limitations, and preferences when it comes to engaging in a discussion or completing an active reading assignment. Then follow the learning activity with a post-discussion or reading reflection using the wrapper concept to get students writing to learn and develop a stronger understand of themselves as learners.

You can also incorporate writing-to-learn activities before students engage in more formalized tasks. Before students write, prompt them to consider their task, their purpose for writing, and their audience. This metacognitive activity gives students an opportunity to practice critical thinking, build empathy, and create specific goals for their writing.

Table 2.2: Exam Wrapper

Exam Wrapper Discussion + Reflection Prompts	
Before the Formative Assessment	After the Formative Assessment
• How prepared do you feel to take this formative assessment? • What are the learning experiences we have had in this class that relate to the focus of this assessment? • Before you share what you know, what areas are you feeling confident in? • Before you share what you know, what specific concepts or skills are you feeling unsure of? • What did you do to prepare for this assessment? How helpful were these strategies?	• If you struggled to share what you have learned, what was the main reason why? • How will the results of this formative assessment impact how you prepare for the summative assessment? • What questions do you still have after reviewing the results of this formative assessment? • Did anything surprise you as you reviewed your results? • Did you notice growth or improvement in any areas? • What are your next steps in terms of acting on the results of this formative assessment?

The "What Really Works Clearinghouse Practice Guide" discusses the importance of prompting students with specific questions and models that help them to reflect on their purpose for writing. The example below shows how a science teacher models her thought process as she sets goals and plans for an essay on animal and plant cells (Table 2.3).[13]

Table 2.3: Thinking Aloud to Model a Planning and Goal-Setting Strategy

Question	Modeled Response
Who is my target audience?	I am writing for a seventh-grade audience, a class that has not yet learned about animal and plant cells. I should be sure to explain terms that the audience may not know.
What goals am I trying to accomplish in my writing?	I need the reader to understand the similarities and differences between animal and plant cells. When planning my essay, I need to think about all of the things I know about animal and plant cells.
What strategy could I use to accomplish my goals?	I could make a Venn diagram to organize my thoughts and compare and contrast those kinds of cells. The headings from the diagram could then be separate points in an outline.
How should I carry out the strategy?	I think I will list the similarities first and then focus on the differences.

Strategy #2: Support Students in Disciplinary Writing

Jennifer Gonzalez is the brilliant facilitator of the *Cult of Pedagogy* podcast. One of her podcasts is titled "7 Easy Ways to Support Student Writing in Any Content Area."[14] We reviewed the strategies and aligned them to UDL and blended learning. Consider which of these practices you can embed within relevant, discipline-specific writing tasks to ensure that students have opportunities to draft, organize, produce, and revise writing that is authentic and relates to the appropriate task, purpose, and audience in your field of study.

Understand how the writing process works. Too often, teachers provide a writing prompt, set a timer, and ask students to write a response, but authentic writing doesn't work like that. Scientists who write scholarly journal articles don't sit down and draft methodology and results in a one-and-done session. In the fine arts, screenwriters don't set a timer and write a screenplay that's guaranteed to win an Oscar. Poets don't sit for an hour and draft a poem. Mathematicians don't write clear mathematical explanations on their first try. In every discipline, writers take time to brainstorm, plan, draft, revise, edit, and publish.

Model. Students need exemplars of what exceptional writing looks like in each discipline. This is a great place to leverage AI solutions, as students can ask for exemplars of authentic writing in each discipline. As an example, I prompted Chat GPT, "What types of writing do mathematicians do?" It very helpfully provided the following response.

> Mathematicians typically write research papers and textbooks. Research papers are typically written to document and share the results of mathematical research, and are typically published in academic journals. Textbooks are written to present the key concepts and techniques of a particular area of mathematics and are used as reference materials or as the basis for classroom instruction. In addition to these types of writing, mathematicians also write expository articles, which are intended to explain mathematical concepts and techniques to a general audience, and may be published in popular science magazines or online.

I then asked for models of expository articles in mathematics and was immediately provided with a sample article, "The Pythagorean Theorem: A Story of Triangles and Circles." As an educator, you of course could research to find models, but we recommend shifting this responsibility to students. Encourage them to find models and exemplars, using all the resources available to them, so they can begin to notice patterns within the content area. We will discuss more about this in chapter 4.

Provide sentence stems. One potential barrier that prevents students from creating authentic writing in each content area may be a lack of awareness of discipline-specific language. We can scaffold this language by providing students with sentence stems. This can be done by asking students to read/review discipline-specific text to pull out common stems.

Write in class. Gonzalez urges teachers to have students write in class, as opposed to writing at home. In addition to boxing out the potential for AI-generated writing, this gives students the opportunity to collaborate with peers, get feedback from peers and teachers, and get support in small-group writing conferences when they struggle.

Make students read their writing out loud. Oftentimes, students will make errors simply because they didn't take the time to proofread. You can provide choices for students to read papers aloud to each other or encourage them to use assistive technology like Google's Read&Write to read their papers out loud to them. As students listen, they can identify potential errors to address during revisions.

Grade with them. Students need to know what high-quality writing looks like within each discipline and how it aligns with expectations on the rubric. One activity that can be done during a station rotation is for groups of students to use the writing rubric to grade the exemplars/models they examined. You can ask them to assume the role of the teacher and grade numerous models while also writing feedback about how well the prompt aligns with expectations in the discipline and to task, purpose, and audience.

Let them rewrite. Writing formally is a process. Once students explore models, review the work of peers, participate in small-group instruction, listen to their writing, and get feedback, they should have opportunities to revise and rework. Writing is not a speed event, and even the most famous writers take numerous drafts to create the highest-quality work.

Strategy #3: Encourage Students to Reflect on Their Writing

Providing time for students to reflect on their writing throughout the year is beneficial because it helps them develop their metacognitive muscles and become more aware of their learning and writing progress. Reflection allows students to identify areas where they have improved and areas they still need to work on. It also helps them set goals and develop strategies to improve their writing, allowing them to become more confident and engaged in the writing process, leading to better outcomes. There are numerous reflection prompts, both writing-to-learn and more formalized, disciplinary literacy prompts you can share with students as they review and reflect on their writing drafts.

You can use the following prompts as writing-to-learn activities and then use the station rotation model to meet with small groups of students. In these groups, they can share their answers while you listen and provide feedback and additional prompts.

- After rereading drafts of your own work, can you see any evidence of your growth as a reader and writer? Please describe what you notice about your performance.
- If you saw growth between your drafts, what do you think is responsible for your progress? Be as specific as you can in your answer.

- If you did not mention this above, to what degree did revising your first draft prepare you to write well on your final draft?[15]

Once you have a reflection prompt, you can use the principles of UDL to provide optional scaffolds to support the reflection process. For example, it may be helpful to create a reflection tool kit for students that contains sentence stems to help prompt their thinking and rubrics to help them assess their progress throughout the writing process by focusing on particular aspects of their writing.

AI-Enhanced Strategy: Student-Crafted Writing Prompts

We've both had the experience of generating writing prompts for students. When teaching *Lord of the Flies*, we asked students to write an argumentative essay responding to a prompt about which boy has the qualities to make the best leader on the island. This checked several boxes in terms of covering our standards, but this prompt was unlikely to excite every student or tap into the aspect of the book they were interested in. Some students may have been mystified by Simon's behavior and wanted to write about what they thought was actually causing him to act the way he did on the island. Other students may have been intrigued by what William Golding was saying about human nature. The point is that the best writing happens when students are interested in the topic.

In most subject areas, when students are given writing assignments, they rarely enjoy agency about what they write about. This lack of meaningful choice negatively impacts the students' motivation to write. Instead of writing from a place of interest or curiosity, they are obligated to complete the assignment to satisfy a requirement and earn a grade. However, if they could think about a topic or

Writing across Disciplines (It's Not Just an English Thing)

unit of study and identify an aspect of that subject that interested or intrigued them, they'd likely be more motivated to put time, energy, and effort into that piece.

One reason teachers may not give students more meaningful decisions in relation to writing is the time it takes for us to generate high-quality writing prompts. AI technology can be incredibly helpful on that front. Elementary teachers could ask a chatbot to generate a collection of writing prompts. For example, we asked ChatGPT to generate a collection of writing prompts that could be used to target the Next Generation Science Standard 3-5-ETS1-2, which states, "Generate and compare multiple solutions to a problem based on how well they meet the criteria and constraints of the design problem." Below is the list of prompts it generated.

- Imagine you are an engineer tasked with designing a new playground. What are some different solutions you could come up with to make the playground fun and safe for everyone who uses it? Compare and contrast the different solutions you came up with, and explain which one you think would be the best choice.
- Your school needs a new recycling program to reduce waste. What are some different solutions you could come up with to encourage people to recycle more? Compare and contrast the different solutions you came up with, and explain which one you think would be the most effective.
- Your class is planning a garden to grow vegetables. What are some different solutions you could come up with to make sure the garden gets enough sunlight and water? Compare and contrast the different solutions you came up with, and explain which one you think would be the best choice for the garden.
- Your family is planning a camping trip, but you only have a limited amount of supplies. What are some different

solutions you could come up with to make sure everyone has everything they need for the trip? Compare and contrast the different solutions you came up with, and explain which one you think would be the most efficient.
- Your town is experiencing a drought, and there is a shortage of water. What are some different solutions you could come up with to conserve water and reduce water usage? Compare and contrast the different solutions you came up with, and explain which one you think would be the most effective in saving water.

In this example, an AI chatbot can save a teacher significant cognitive energy by generating a collection of prompts they can provide learners to choose from. And if you are thinking, *But how do I support students as they complete the actual writing if they might be responding to so many different prompts?* Well, that's where UDL and blended learning are key!

Teachers can use a chatbot to generate sentence stems in seconds to support students in responding to the various prompts. They can also use the station rotation model to group students by their chosen prompt and provide small-group support and feedback as they work. They can also create an expository or information writing playlist with different prompts and different embedded supports to allow students to self-pace through the playlist with the prompt they are most interested in writing about.

Secondary students can play a more active role in this process by using an AI chatbot to generate and refine their own writing prompts. Instead of relying on the teacher to generate the writing prompts, students can become active agents in the writing process, learning how to craft their own prompts in relation to a specific topic, subject, or issue. The process might look something like the one outlined in Table 2.4.

Table 2.4: Student-Generated Writing Prompts Using AI Chatbots

Student-Generated Writing Prompts Using AI Chatbots	
Step 1: Introduce the Topic and Writing Style	The teacher introduces the topic, subject, issue, and writing genre (e.g., narrative, informational, argumentative). The teacher may also provide examples of writing prompts for the class to analyze, as discussed in chapter 4.
Step 2: Brainstorm and Collaborate	Students discuss the topic, subject, or issue and brainstorm prompt ideas that fit within the given category or style aligned with target standards. What aspects of the topic are they most interested in? What types of prompts align with the writing genre and standard?
Step 3: Submit Ideas to an AI Chatbot	Students submit their writing prompt ideas to an AI technology tool, like ChatGPT, for feedback and refinement. This positions the students to think about what keywords will likely generate writing prompts of interest.
Step 4: Share and Select	After students receive feedback from the AI chatbot, they can share their ideas with their peers or in small groups. That way, if one student has a prompt that other classmates are interested in using, they can select their favorite student-generated prompt and benefit from their peers' ideas.
Step 5: Teacher Feedback	Teachers can review the prompts students have generated or selected to ensure they are high quality, appropriate, and meet the assignment's learning objectives.

Students using AI to generate writing prompts and assignment topics will quickly discover that the quality of the ideas, words, and questions they input into an AI chatbot will impact the quality of the output. This process positions the students to think critically about the subjects they are learning about and the types of writing they are being asked to produce, which engages their higher-order thinking skills.

Wrap-Up

Too often, writing is banished to the halls of English language arts and humanities departments. Certainly, writing is assigned in numerous subjects but is not necessarily taught. We argue there is incredible value in teaching writing across the curriculum by prompting students with writing-to-learn activities as well as assessments that encourage disciplinary literacy. When writing is implemented across the curriculum, using writing-to-learn models, student learning and motivation increase. This is where UDL and blended learning come in as valuable frameworks. To support this approach, we offer the following strategies:

- Strategy #1: Assign Daily Writing-to-Learn Activities
- Strategy #2: Support Students in Disciplinary Writing
- Strategy #3: Encourage Students to Reflect on Their Writing
- AI-Enhanced Strategy: Student-Crafted Writing Prompts

Reflect/Discuss

1. College and career-ready standards discuss the importance of students identifying a task, purpose, and audience for writing. How often do you provide students with a prompt and ask them to reflect on the task, purpose, and audience? How could the strategies in this chapter help you to make that process more explicit?

2. What writing-to-learn activities could you incorporate into your existing practice by using or adapting the concept of a learning journal?
3. Reflect on your content area. What does it mean to be a writer in your field? How can you design prompts so students can share their learning in an authentic writing assessment that prepares them for work in your content area?
4. How can you facilitate the process of guiding students in developing their own writing prompts? What would this look like in your class?

Putting It into Action

1. Craft a writing prompt in your content area.
2. After you share the prompt with students, ask them to reflect on the questions in the table below and write the answers as a non-graded writing-to-learn activity.
3. Ask students to share their responses with peers to reflect on different strategies.
4. Provide feedback in station rotations so students can refine their strategy before beginning the writing process.

Question	Modeled Response
Who is my target audience?	
What goals am I trying to accomplish in my writing?	
What strategy could I use to accomplish my goals?	
How should I carry out the strategy?	

3

Blended Instruction to Boot the Sage off the Stage

Love Made Me Buy a Fanny Pack

Catlin I am one of the twenty-three million Americans who adopted a dog during the pandemic. In April 2020, I reached out to North Bay German Shepherd Rescue, the organization I used to adopt two previous shepherds. On their website, there was a beautiful two-year-old female shepherd, Lyla Grace, who needed a home. After going back and forth with my adoption liaison, the woman boarding Lyla brought her to my house so we could meet to see if it was a good fit.

When they arrived, Lyla jumped out of the car and ran to me. She jumped up, paws on my chest (we'd have to work on that), and gave me a big wet kiss on the cheek. I was smitten. She was sweet, energetic, and very curious. As she sniffed around my backyard, I chatted with her foster mom. She told me Lyla was the sweetest dog she'd ever fostered, but she had leash aggression. Apparently, she had been returned from three different homes because the people who adopted her could not handle her on the leash. I was not alarmed by this information. Instead, thanks to my competitive nature, I took this as a challenge, and I felt I was up to that challenge. A big part of the reason I wanted to adopt a younger dog was so she could join me on my daily 4.5-mile walk. I would not be giving this dog back if I decided to adopt her.

Since I didn't know anything about leash aggression, I decided to google it. I read articles and watched half a dozen YouTube videos on the topic. I understood that it typically stems from insecurity and saw videos of people walking dogs that lost their minds when passing other people. A few of the videos provided tips and strategies for managing those moments. One dog trainer recommended treat training, so I bought a Costco bag of dehydrated duck jerky for dogs, cut the chunks into small pieces, and put them in a plastic bag. Then I did something I had sworn in the past I would never do! I, Catlin Tucker, bought a fanny pack. Love makes you do crazy things! I packed it with poop bags and dog treats, cinched it around my waist, and took off for my first walk with Lyla.

The walk started great. Lyla trotted by my side, and we practiced a few techniques I had seen on the YouTube video to get her attention. They worked, I rewarded her, and I thought, *What was wrong with all those other people who gave Lyla back? This was so easy!*

No sooner had this snarky thought run through my head when I saw another dog walker. I took a deep breath, got a treat ready, and was prepared to use the technique I'd learned to get her attention. It did *not* go well. Lyla lost it! She could not have cared less about me, my technique, or the treats. She was lunging, barking, and yanking the leash violently. And she is a big dog, weighing in at seventy-five pounds—she almost knocked me off my feet! I was in shock. The experience left me shaking, my heart racing, and my body coursing with adrenaline. We had two other incidents on that walk, though I was smart enough to cross the street as soon as I spotted another dog or a bike (since people riding bikes elicited the same response).

I realized the YouTube videos had been useful in helping me to understand leash aggression, but they were not going to help me to train Lyla so she could gain the confidence she needed to remain calm on our walks. That evening, I signed Lyla and me up for dog training lessons. I needed an expert to show me what to do, provide corrective feedback, and create a safe space where we could pass other dogs while I practiced the techniques I was learning. It took three months of lessons and daily walks to practice on our own before Lyla's leash aggression began to fade and the idea of walking her no longer gave me hot sweats.

Now, two and a half years later, Lyla is a dream to walk. We pass dogs, and she barely acknowledges them! I love our daily walks together.

For some explanations, videos are great! They can provide a helpful overview of information or demonstrate a process or strategy. However, for more challenging tasks, like retraining an insecure dog, you may need more than a video. You may need an expert who can provide individual or small-group support, just as the experienced dog trainer was able to demonstrate techniques and then observe me, providing feedback as I attempted to apply them. The same is true for learning in a classroom. Some information can be transferred effectively and efficiently using a video, while other, more complex concepts, strategies, and skills benefit from a teacher leading small-group or individual instruction and a modeling session.

Research and Reality

Writing is one of the most cognitively challenging tasks students are asked to do in school. When writing, students must make myriad decisions about word choice, spelling, sentence structure, organization, transitions, and tone. Even the commonly assigned task of summarizing an assigned reading places significant demands on a student's working memory as they attempt to take what they have learned about a topic or text, then evaluate the topic or text to identify the most important point or parts, select those elements, and describe them concisely and accurately.[1]

The National Assessment of Educational Progress (NAEP) published the Nation's Report Card on Writing, revealing that only about 25 percent of students performed at a proficient level in writing. The data for twelfth-grade students specifically highlights the disparity in achievement between white students and students of color: 34 percent of white students scored proficient or above, compared to 9 percent of black students and 12 percent of Latinx students.[2] The National Commission on Writing has designated writing as "a neglected skill in American schools" and shows that current approaches are not addressing the achievement gap or helping the majority of students to reach proficiency.[3]

A meta-analysis of twenty-eight studies on writing instruction found that although some teachers use a writing program to guide their writing instruction, most do not, and concluded that "writing instruction in most classrooms is inadequate."[4] Research on current writing practices in the United States and globally indicates that the majority of teachers are not dedicating sufficient time to teach students how to write or using adequate instructional practices, that students are not writing frequently enough, and that digital tools are not being utilized to support the writing process.[5] When you consider these inadequacies alongside new AI technologies that can compose structurally and substantively strong pieces of writing in response to any prompt, it's clear that educators need to reevaluate their approach to writing instruction.

The whole-group, teacher-led, sage-on-the-stage approach to instruction presents myriad barriers that may make it challenging for students to access the information being presented when teachers are explicitly teaching writing strategies. Students may not have the background knowledge or vocabulary to understand the instruction. The pace that the teacher is presenting information may be too fast or too slow for students. Students may have attention or auditory processing challenges that interfere with their ability to take in and process the information. Other students may simply be distracted, not feeling well, or absent, missing the instruction entirely.[6] These are just a few barriers that UDL encourages teachers to identify and attempt to remove through intentional design.

The whole-group approach to instruction also positions students as receivers of information and relegates them to a passive role in the lecture or mini-lesson.[7] If students are spending significant time listening passively to teachers explain information, it's no wonder that 49 percent of students surveyed said "school was boring."[8] When students are not actively engaged, or their specific needs are not being met by instruction, the experience is bound to be perceived as boring.

Despite the challenges associated with whole-group, teacher-led writing instruction, students need explicit instruction on *how* to write. They must understand the purpose of a piece of writing. Is it meant to inform, persuade, or entertain? They need to know how to structure a piece of writing to convey their ideas clearly and cogently. For example, if they are writing a compare and contrast, they need to decide between a point-by-point or block structure. When writing a lab report, they need to know what sections are needed and in what order they should appear. Then there are issues of mechanics, style, and tone. Writing is complex and multifaceted, which is why students must receive writing instruction and support across disciplines.

Not all writing instruction is created equal. The What Works Clearinghouse provides a research brief about evidence-based practices that improve adolescent writing.[9] Only a single practice has strong evidence: explicitly teaching appropriate writing strategies using a model-practice-reflect instructional cycle. During model-practice-reflect, students observe a specific strategy, practice it on their own or with peers, and evaluate their writing and use of the strategy.

As teachers think about providing writing instruction, we encourage them to look beyond the whole-group, teacher-led, teacher-paced model and instead use blended learning models to ensure that students have access to the model-practice-reflect instructional cycle. The previous approach may feel efficient because it lets the teacher say something one time and then move on, but it is rarely effective. Instead, as teachers think about their writing instruction, we encourage them to ask the questions "Am I planning to say the same thing the same way to everyone?" and "Is everyone going to examine the same model?" The answer to these questions should determine whether a teacher uses the flipped classroom model to present instruction with a video recording or pulls the instruction into a small-group setting at their teacher-led station using the station rotation model.

Let's imagine you are about to start your first extended writing assignment of the year with students. It may be an essay, a lab report, or an explanation about how they solved a mathematical problem. You will probably explain the importance of a topic sentence or thesis statement, where it goes in a paragraph, and how to structure the response. You will likely explain this the same way for everyone. This is a great example of content that would be best presented in a short video since everyone needs to hear it, and we can tell you from years of teaching writing they will need to hear it again and again and again! Instead of spending class time reviewing the same explanation multiple times, teachers can save time (and their sanity!) by presenting this information in a video that students can watch as many times as they need during a school year.

In a survey about teachers' perceptions of the flipped classroom and using video instruction, teachers reported that flipping instruction with video "creates time for varied instructional techniques, including active learning and higher order thinking, along with increased student-to-teacher interaction."[10] Exactly! We are not saying teachers should use video for all instruction; instead, we encourage teachers to use video instruction strategically to create more time and space for teacher-student interactions in the form of small-group or individualized instruction.

There are more complex and nuanced aspects of the writing process that benefit from small-group instruction, where the teacher can differentiate the explanation and models they use to help students understand how to approach a complex part of the writing process. For example, analyzing textual evidence is challenging for many students. Too often, they fall into the habit of simply restating a quote or summarizing a portion of the text, instead of digging into the textual evidence to break it down and demonstrate how it supports their claims. Because it's a challenging writing skill, we suggest you pull this instruction into your teacher-led station as part of the station rotation model. That way, you can select textual evidence at different levels of complexity to demonstrate the skill of analyzing a text to support a point. You can also allow students to work alone or with a partner as they practice in your small group. You can listen, observe, and support as needed, making additional scaffolds (e.g., sentence frames and deconstructed examples) available to students who need more help.

Strategy #1: Flipping Writing Instruction with Video

The flipped classroom model inverts the traditional approach to instruction and application, presenting information via video recordings so more class time can be used for practice and application. This model frees the teacher from feeling pressure to stand at the front of the class and lead whole-group instruction, allowing them to spend more time working with small groups or individual students.

Flipping writing instruction is a powerful strategy with benefits for learners and teachers. First, if we think about many of the barriers that make it challenging for students to acquire information when it is presented live (e.g., pacing, absence), video can help to mitigate or even eliminate some of those barriers. When information is presented using a video, students can manipulate that information in ways that aren't possible during a live lecture or mini-lesson. They may be able to add closed captioning and slow down the pace of a video. They can rewind, rewatch, and pause to look up a word or google a reference if they lack the vocabulary or background knowledge to understand the content. This shift in control from teacher to learner can effectively remove barriers that make acquiring new information challenging and positively impact the students' confidence, motivation, and attitude.[11]

Second, flipping instruction with video saves teachers precious class time since they do not have to spend time presenting these foundational explanations or lose instructional minutes repeating instruction. Anyone who has taught students how to write knows that they often need to hear explanations and see models more than once. The beauty of short instructional videos is that they are available any time students would benefit from rewatching them.

There are some important design considerations to remember when creating an instructional writing video.

- Keep explanations short and sweet!
- Get intentional about the visual components of your video (e.g., slide deck).
- Clearly communicate your expectations for how students should engage with the video.
- Provide meaningful choices about how students capture their learning.

One mistake we have both made is recording videos that are too long and trying to cover too much information. In a study of student engagement with instructional videos, the length of the video had the biggest impact on student engagement.[12] That same study made an argument for six minutes being the sweet spot for video length. So, instead of recording one video explaining how to structure an argumentative or informational paragraph, which can take upward of fifteen minutes (neither one of us was able to do it in less than twelve), break down the individual parts of the writing process and record a separate video for each part of the paragraph (e.g., claim, evidence). This will help you stay closer to that sweet spot of six minutes.

Along with being easier for students to stay engaged with, shorter videos also become valuable resources during the feedback process. As you read through a piece of student writing, you may realize they need to spend time developing a claim, selecting stronger textual evidence or research, or expanding and developing their analysis or explanation. Instead of directing students to rewatch one long video, you can provide a link in their feedback to a video on a specific element of their writing they need to develop or rework. These shorter videos can provide repeat exposure to the specific aspect of the writing process they need to review before they revise. So, the moral of the story: keep your focus narrow and video length limited.

The next tip when creating instructional writing videos is to be intentional about what students see in your video. Avoid huge blocks of text; instead, opt for bullets and key phrases. This can be tricky with a writing instruction video and demands a higher level of intentionality as you design your slide deck or the visual component of your video. The goal is to avoid having students copying down unnecessary information that may distract them from listening to your explanation. Because the instruction is focused on writing, you will likely show students examples of writing to make a point or highlight a technique; however, you want to explicitly tell them in the video what information needs to be copied into their notes, graphic organizer, or concept map and what is simply an example.

In addition to being mindful of the volume of words on your screen when recording a video, teachers need to be clear about the expectations around how students should document their thinking as they watch the video. This documentation serves as evidence of completion for teachers who send videos home with students or assign a video lesson in an online station in a rotation. The note-taking strategy is an opportunity for you to provide meaningful choices about *how* students capture their notes as they watch the video. Some students may prefer taking traditional notes or Cornell notes; others may gravitate to more visual forms of note-taking, like graphic organizers, concept maps, or sketchnotes. You can use a choice board, like the one pictured in Figure 3.1, to offer students the choice of multiple note-taking strategies.

 Figure 3.1: Flipped Writing Video Note-Taking Choice Board

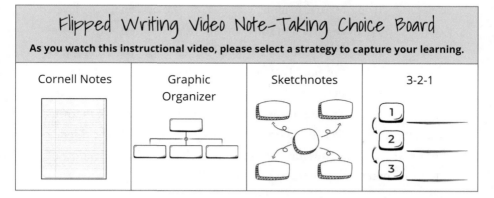

Videos are more effective if students mentally engage with the information by capturing their learning and answering questions or engaging in a conversation about the content of the video. This helps keep them engaged instead of slipping into a passive consumptive role. You can invite students who watch the video in class to decide if they would prefer to watch it on their own or watch with a partner, pausing periodically to discuss the video and talk through the information they add to the notes. This simple option can provide students with peer support if they feel that would be helpful.

Strategy #2: Differentiated Writing Instruction with the Station Rotation Model

The station rotation model rotates students through online and offline learning activities. There are three types of stations: a) teacher-led, b) online, and c) offline. A station rotation lesson typically has three or four stations that students move through during a class or two, depending on the length of the class.

The teacher-led station creates time for small-group writing instruction that can be differentiated or needs-based. If you focus on selecting strong textual evidence, analyzing the evidence, or developing explanations, you can differentiate that experience in several ways. For example, if you want to help students identify strong textual evidence to support their points, you can present a statement or claim and challenge some groups to explore a text by looking for quotes or evidence they think are particularly strong. Ask them to explain their choices. For a group that may struggle to find evidence in a text, you can present a statement or claim and a collection of quotes. Then challenge them to work on their own or with a partner to rank the evidence from strongest to weakest. After they have completed that challenge, you can facilitate a group conversation about why they ranked the textual evidence in a particular order.

Similarly, teachers can use the "I do, we do, pairs do, you do" gradual release to guide students through the process of pulling the evidence apart to explain its significance, whether they are analyzing evidence from an experiment in science, research for an argumentative essay in history, or supporting quotes for an informational essay in English. Teachers can use evidence at different levels of complexity and have sentence stems available for students to reference as they work to analyze it (Table 3.1).

Table 3.1: Gradual Release Model for Teacher-Led Station

Gradual Release Model for Teacher-Led Station	
I do	Teacher models the process for students, using a think-aloud to help students understand their thought process and the steps involved in completing a particular task.
We do	Teacher engages students in working through another example as a group, gently correcting misconceptions and highlighting strong contributions.
Pairs do	Teacher strategically pairs students to work through another example. While pairs are working, the teacher listens and observes to identify the students who are ready for independent practice and those who may need additional instruction and support from the teacher.
You do	Teacher releases students ready for individual practice, providing tasks at a level of complexity and rigor appropriate for them.

If diagnostic data or student performance on a writing assignment indicates that different groups of students would benefit from instruction on different aspects of the writing process, teachers can group students by need and provide entirely different instruction for each group at the teacher-led station. This recognizes the variability in a classroom and ensures that all students are receiving the instruction and support they need to make progress toward firm, standards-aligned learning goals.

Not only does the station rotation model create the time and space for teachers to work directly with a smaller subset of the larger class, it gives students at the online and offline stations more control over the pace of their learning. The online station could be a video lesson introducing students to the next aspect of the writing process or providing instruction on a technical element of writing, like introducing or citing quotes. Alternatively, it could be a writing station where students have class time to work on their reports, essays, or papers. The offline station could encourage a peer-review process or ask students to analyze exemplars to understand the essential elements of a piece of writing to construct a simple rubric (more on this in chapter 4). Figure 3.2 shows an example of a writing-focused station rotation.

 Figure 3.2: Writing-Focused Station Rotation Lesson

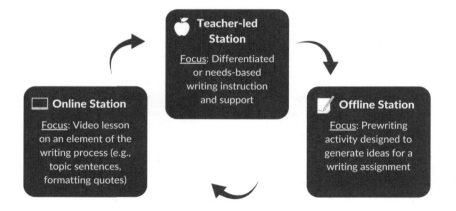

AI-Enhanced Strategy: Use Adaptive Learning Platforms to Differentiate and Personalize Instruction

Numerous adaptive learning platforms can be used in an online station so that students can access targeted and personalized instruction in writing. For example, many schools and districts use solutions like NoRedInk. NoRedInk offers authentic assessments, adaptive practice, and personalized content to help improve student writing.

Teachers can assign pathways, which are personalized playlists, to students focused on specific goals (Figure 3.3). Each pathway has numerous options and choices for students to personalize their learning experience. For example, one pathway is focused on embedding evidence into body paragraphs. At the beginning of the path, there is a note about mastery: "To master a topic, you must demonstrate full understanding of that topic. Mastery is not about answering a set number of questions or spending a certain number of minutes on NoRedInk. Instead, mastery-based practice builds a tailored set of questions to meet your needs." The pathway, or playlist, allows students to work at their own pace and demonstrate mastery at pre-determined checkpoints before moving to the next step in the path.

Adaptive learning platforms can provide targeted and individualized instruction that meets the specific needs and goals of each learner. Personalized pathways allow students to work at their own pace and demonstrate mastery at pre-determined checkpoints before moving to the next step in the path. This approach helps students make progress toward firm, standards-aligned writing goals and promotes a sense of autonomy and ownership over their learning journey. Personalizing content and assessments empowers students to improve their skills and reach their full potential.

Figure 3.3: No Red Ink Learning Playlist

Part 1: Evaluating Evidence

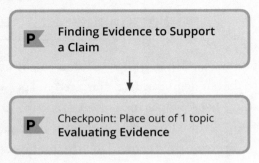

Part 2: Providing Strong Context for Literary Evidence

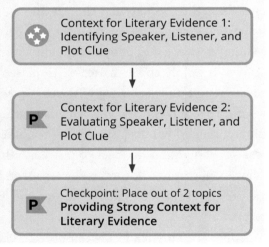

Part 3: Providing Strong Context for Nonfiction Evidence

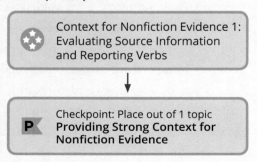

Wrap-Up

Too often, teachers design writing instruction using one-size-fits-all practices, which assume that all students need the same instruction at the same time and at the same pace. Given the variability in student writing, this is not a model that challenges and supports all learners. Instead, this chapter encourages teachers to think of the purpose of writing instruction and use a blended learning model that best aligns with the purpose of instruction to meet the needs of all learners. If writing instruction is focused on providing explicit guidance to learners, the flipped classroom model is best. Not only can students personalize their viewing experience, but they can view the instruction multiple times, and if necessary, you can provide the link to the video as feedback on formative assessments. When formative assessments indicate the need for targeted, explicit instruction, a station rotation allows teachers to provide differentiated instruction in small groups while other students engage in offline and online stations with their peers. Here are some of the key strategies that can be used to promote effective writing instruction and support diverse learners:

- Strategy #1: Flipping Writing Instruction with Video
- Strategy #2: Differentiated Writing Instruction with the Station Rotation Model
- AI-Enhanced Strategy: Use Adaptive Learning Platforms to Differentiate and Personalize Instruction

Reflect/Discuss

1. How do you currently approach writing instruction? How much time in class do you dedicate to instruction versus supporting students as they write?
2. What barriers do you think might make it challenging for students to access information during a live lecture or mini-lesson?

3. What explanations or instruction do you find yourself repeating multiple times over the course of a school year? How might shifting these explanations online with video positively impact you and your students?
4. How often do you provide needs-based or differentiated instruction? How might you use the station rotation model to increase the frequency of these approaches to instruction?

Putting It into Practice

Step 1: Think about the writing students do in your class and brainstorm the aspects of the writing instruction that you tend to explain or model the same way for all students. Once you've identified these, think about the more complex and nuanced aspects of writing that benefit from differentiated small-group instruction. Complete the table below.

Flipped Instruction with Video	Small-Group Instruction
In the space below, brainstorm all the parts of the writing process you present the same way for everyone.	In the space below, brainstorm the more complex or nuanced aspects of the writing process that students struggle with and that would benefit from targeted instruction.

Step 2: Select one item from your flipped column and use the tips presented in this chapter to create a short writing instruction video. Remember, your video doesn't need to be perfect!

Step 3: Select one item from your small-group instruction column and design a teacher-led station using the gradual release model presented in this chapter. Think about how you can differentiate the content or process at this station to meet the needs of all students.

Step 4: Share your video and your small-group instruction lesson with a colleague or your personal learning network for feedback. Reflect on the feedback and revise as needed.

4

Deconstructing and Analyzing Writing Samples

Deconstructing Cabinet Faces

Katie   "Ohmigosh! I loooooove it!" You hear it all the time about interior design—during the big reveal on a home improvement show, through the comments on an Instagram post, or maybe you yourself have muttered the words as you see a friend's new home or scroll through Pinterest. Kitchens in particular—the heart of the home—get a lot of attention with ooohs and ahhs all around. But when you ask, "What do you love about it?" you'll often hear things like "The gold handles and how bright it is!" or "That light is amazing!" The details that really make beautiful design what it is—the stuff that designers painstakingly make decisions about—are often lost on people like me.

In full disclosure, I am one of those people who ooohs and ahhs without any real understanding of why I like what I like. During COVID, I decided that my kitchen needed a refresh. When we bought the home, the backsplash in the kitchen was maroon, which made the whole room look dark, and there was a kidney-shaped countertop that sliced the kitchen in half. I wanted a lighter, brighter, more open-concept kitchen, and luckily, I have a sister, Lindie, who is a natural genius in interior design.

Unfortunately, from the beginning, she was ready to pummel me because of my complete ignorance of all things design. My entire plan was to find a single picture on Pinterest that I liked and then send it to her so she could help design a kitchen that looked like that. How hard could that be? Turns out, there are about a million decisions to make when renovating a kitchen. Who knew? Once Lindie had my vision, she went to work measuring and designing. Once the layout was complete, the cabinet questions started. Now, before this intervention, if you were to ask me what kind of cabinets I wanted, my answer would have been white. That's it. In fact, when she said, "So, tell me more about the cabinets you want," that is the exact answer I gave her.

There was silence on the other end of the phone. She recovered: "OK, are you leaning toward a bright white or something creamier, like Benjamin Moore's Swiss Coffee?" Crickets. She took my lack of response as an invitation to keep the questions coming.

"And which cabinet face do you like? And what material are you going to use? And what do you want for paneling and hardware and lighting?"

"I literally don't even know what any of that means," I said. "What are the cheapest ones?" I think she may have started to hyperventilate.

As I drafted this chapter, I reminded her about Cabinetgate and my utter lack of respect for cabinet carpentry. I asked her to remind me of the differences in cabinet faces, and she launched into action, discussing all the virtues of various cabinet styles. I couldn't keep up so I asked her to send me an email. If you want to know what my sister is like, the following excerpt is an excellent sneak peek. (Love you, Linny!)

> For starters, there are four major types of kitchen cabinet face: frameless (or "euro" overlay, sometimes also called full

access), partial overlay, full overlay, and full inset. In modern kitchens, you see very little partial overlay these days. If you look at a kitchen and think, "gosh, that looks like the 80s or 90s," you are likely witnessing partial overlay. In this facing type, you see a reveal of about 1 inch or more of cabinet frame tucked back behind each of the kitchen cabinet doors. Oftentimes, it fails to create consistent spacing and a line to help direct the eye.

Full overlay, making its big trend debut in the early 2000s, steps it up a notch by revealing less of that kitchen cabinet frame (maybe only 1/2 inch) and helps modernize a kitchen. We still see a lot of full overlay cabinetry in today's kitchens. But to get a cleaner look, something that many viewers won't even notice but will somehow add that extra "WHY DOES THIS LOOK SO GOOD?!?!" feeling is the euro overlay. These cabinets, popularized in Europe, don't have a face frame. While the frame helps stabilize the cabinet box and adds more rigidity to it, there is something definitely beautiful about the streamlined look of frameless cabinets. There are very small gaps between doors and cabinets (more like 1/8"), creating a much more consistent look, and those details can totally change the look of a space.

Last is the crème de la crème of cabinetry—the full inset. In these cabinets, which are often custom-built for fine homes, the door is fully set within the cabinet frame. Building these cabinets takes a tremendous amount of precision, but usually, you don't have quite as much access to your storage space as you would in a frameless cabinet.

There you have it, folks—the crème de la crème of cabinetry is the full inset. Now, as much as I love teasing my sister, our whole interaction is a great analogy for deconstructing writing exemplars in your content area. Because like it or not, I can now walk into a kitchen and comment on the cabinet construction, which gives me a much greater appreciation for the thoughtfulness of designers and contractors.

Oftentimes, we share models or exemplars with our students, and like me, they say, "I like that one," or "That one is really good," without knowing exactly what makes the writing high-quality. As instructors, we know there is incredible power in helping students deconstruct the elements of disciplinary writing so they can analyze, compare and contrast, and decide for themselves what constitutes the "crème de la crème."

Research and Reality

Exemplars are key writing examples chosen to demonstrate a level of quality, and they can be instrumental in supporting students throughout the writing process. In the 1980s, Professor Royce Sadler identified three conditions necessary for students to improve the quality of their work: 1) students need the capacity to monitor the quality of their own work, 2) students must understand what high-quality work is, and be able to compare/contrast that work with their own with objectivity, and 3) they must have strategies that they can apply to revise their own work.[1] For students to understand what high-quality writing looks like, we need to provide examples of the types of writing we expect them to produce within each discipline.

Simply sharing exemplars and models is not enough. Research is clear that this results in only modest gains. Writing samples need to be paired with explicit instruction on how to analyze the text, and students need time for reflection so they can develop strategies to apply to their own writing.[2] Writing quality increases exponentially when students learn to write while developing self-management skills like setting their own writing goals; self-prompting with appropriate strategies to plan, draft, revise, and edit; and self-regulating their performance. These outcomes align with the goal of UDL and blended learning to create more motivated, engaged, expert learners who take responsibility for their own learning.

Regardless of what level you teach, it can be a valuable exercise to show students what they are working toward. Imagine that you are asking elementary students to write a script for a TED Talk to explain an idea. It may be tempting to create a graphic organizer where they brainstorm what they are passionate about and how they could share a story about that passion, without sharing transcripts of TED Talks with accompanying videos.

But to help students better understand what makes a strong script and performance, we recommend first sharing the TED Talk speaker guide so students can see the expectations for the most brilliant minds in the world. Next, students can choose a TED Talk that is interesting to them and read/listen to the script as an example. You may think, *That is outrageous! My fourth-grade students aren't writing scripts as sophisticated as Bill Gates, Sir Ken Robinson, and Chimamanda Ngozi Adichie.* We would like to add "yet." In any field, students need to see examples of authentic writing so they can set goals for closing the distance between their current level of performance and true excellence.

In "Austin's Butterfly," one of our favorite educational videos that examines the power of exemplars to drive student awareness of high-quality work, critique, reflection, and feedback, Models of Excellence curator Ron Berger shares a project from Austin, a first-grade student in Boise, Idaho, who created a scientific drawing of a butterfly for a note card that would be sold to raise funds for butterfly habitats.[3] To illuminate the efficacy of critique and multiple drafts, Berger shows six drafts of Austin's drawing to students and elicits their kind, specific, and helpful critiques as they consider how each draft could be improved. The progress from primitive first draft to impressive final draft is a powerful message for educators:

we often settle for low-quality work because we underestimate the capacity of students to create great work. With time, clarity, critique, and support, students are capable of much more than we imagine. If you haven't seen this video yet, we highly recommend watching and sharing it with students.

Both Universal Design for Learning (UDL) and blended learning can help teachers incorporate exemplars into writing instruction while they provide guidance and support for students to analyze these models to better understand what high-quality writing is and how they can create it.

Strategy #1: Use Exemplars from a Variety of Sources

In chapter 2, we briefly discussed the importance of sharing exemplars with students and mentioned using AI solutions, like ChatGPT, to generate examples for students to analyze. But these may not provide the high level of quality a prompt requires (fingers crossed). In the spirit of UDL, there are numerous additional options and choices for curating exemplars in your content area.

- **Authentic written work in the field.** Each field of study has authentic texts. Sharing these with students can help them to understand what high-quality work looks like. For example, in a science course, you may share white papers from scientific conferences, analyze peer-reviewed research papers that document scientific insights, explore pamphlets from local hospitals, and/or read articles in publications like *Scientific American*. In mathematics, you may read mathematical explanations written by mathematicians, cost-benefit analyses, lecture notes from math professors at local universities, or articles from *The American Mathematical Monthly* or the

National Council of Teachers of Mathematics (NCTM)'s *Mathematics Teacher*. Physical education teachers can review personal training plans from local trainers and articles in *Muscle and Fitness*. Teachers in vocational-technical fields can share project proposals and manuals. And you don't have to look for these artifacts alone. Empower students to reach out to local professionals in your field and ask what kind of writing they do in their jobs. You can provide an email template and sentence stems, and students can work together to curate exemplars from professionals that can be used to set goals for writing.

- **Past student work.** Many teachers are in the habit of handing back all student work, but wait! Ask students who create exceptional work if you can make a digital copy and share it with future classes. You may even want to ask them to record a short audio or video introducing themselves and the assignment. This provides another explanation of the assignment and allows students to see that success is possible. Ensure you have a diverse representation of students so all students can see scholars who share their identities.

- **Dogfooding.** Jennifer Gonzalez produced a podcast episode, "Dogfooding: How Often Do You Do Your Own Assignments?" She argues that teachers should dogfood, or complete their own assignments, to set expectations and write clearer directions. In the accompanying blog, she writes:

    > Dogfooding an assignment allows you to build a prototype of a finished product, which can work wonders for helping students understand what's expected of them. This is especially important with larger projects, when students will be spending days or weeks putting together the pieces of some final presentation or artifact, or when the product

you have in mind is something students have never really seen. So if, for example, you would like students to write and perform satirical skits in which they parody some significant event in history, go ahead and create one yourself first. Not only will this help you better appreciate the scope of what you're asking students to do, it will give them a much clearer target to aim for.[4]

Strategy #2: Identify Key Attributes or Essential Elements

Once you have exemplars, it is important to scaffold how to deconstruct them so that students can learn more about text structure, the attributes of different types of writing, and how an author's style contributes to a text's meaning. Given that all students have to learn to write for task, purpose, and audience, it can be a helpful exercise for students to analyze each exemplar through those lenses. We adapted Table 4.1 from What Works Clearinghouse's "Teaching Secondary Students to Write Effectively" (see chapter 2 for a discussion of this resource in regard to prompts) to help students reflect on the writer's task, purpose, and audience.[5]

Table 4.1: Analyzing Exemplars for Task, Purpose, and Audience

Question	How do you know? Share specific techniques/evidence to support your answer.
Who is the target audience?	
What are the writer's goals with their writing?	
What strategies did the author use to accomplish their goals?	
Which strategy can you apply in your own writing?	

Once students can identify the task, purpose, and audience, they can examine the text structure. The three main writing genres are argumentative, informative, and narrative. The anchor standards in Writing for the Common Core Standards identify the following genre-specific goals.

- Write arguments to support claims in an analysis of substantive topics or texts, using valid reasoning and relevant and sufficient evidence.
- Write informative/explanatory texts to examine and convey complex ideas and information clearly and accurately through the effective selection, organization, and analysis of content.
- Write narratives to develop experiences or events using effective literary techniques, well-chosen details, and well-structured sequences.

Each of these genres can be analyzed for task, purpose, and audience, but when it comes to identifying text structures, there are differences. Table 4.2 identifies common text structures by genre.[6] You can use or adapt this table to include additional text structures from your discipline.

Table 4.2: Text Structures for Different Genres of Writing

Argumentative	Informative	Narrative
Analysis	Definition	Descriptive
Compare and contrast	Description	Sequential/linear
Cause and effect	Explanation	Non-linear
Evaluation	Analysis	
Problem/solution	Compare and contrast	
	Cause and effect	
	Procedural/sequential	
	Hypothesis/experiment	

In addition to differing text structures, each genre of writing has unique attributes, which are identified in Table 4.3.[7]

Table 4.3: Attributes in Different Genres of Writing

Argumentative	Informative	Narrative
A debatable and supportable claim	Clear thesis statement	Establishes a narrative line or theme that is carried through the narrative
Logical reasoning to support your claim	Presents and applies relevant information with accuracy	
Sound evidence and examples to justify the reasoning	Explains key information with sufficient detail	Employs stylistic devices to develop a sense of time, place, or character
Reasonable projections		
Concessions and rebuttals		

Explicitly teaching these attributes and providing opportunities for students to identify them while deconstructing texts will allow learners to create schemas for that type of writing in their own practice. Using the principles of UDL, you can send students on a scavenger hunt, either alone, with a partner, or in small groups, to find these attributes in a text under study, or they can look for them in their own writing. This work could be done as a station in a rotation or an activity in a writing playlist.

Strategy #3: Embrace Non-examples, Too

Although it's important to share high-quality examples of discipline-specific writing, it is also valuable for students to explore non-examples. In resources provided to support faculty, Metropolitan State University of Denver discusses the purpose of using non-examples. They prompt instructors to show students less-than-satisfactory projects, highlighting why they do not meet expectations. Or better yet, to ask students to explain why they don't meet expectations.[8] This is an especially powerful exercise after they have examined exemplars, as this will help them identify differences that will support them in drafting success criteria for their own work.

When we were both practicing English/language arts teachers, we had to prepare students to succeed in standardized assessments. Tests like SmarterBalanced, PARCC, the SAT, and the ACT have numerous examples of student work at many different levels of proficiency. Here are some of the ways we used these examples and non-examples.

- Collect numerous examples of varying quality, then have students review the rubric and put them in order from the strongest to the one that needs the most support.
- Have students compare and contrast an exemplar and a non-example and note similarities and differences.

- After exploring non-examples, have students compare and contrast their own writing to the non-example. What similarities do they notice that would benefit from a revision?
- Provide students with a non-example and task them with revising it so it better aligns with the rubric.

If you curate your own collection of examples and non-examples, you may be able to use or adapt some of these strategies in your own practice.

Strategy #4: Create a Simple Rubric

Constructing a rubric with learners that highlights success criteria and their essential attributes is a valuable way to build a shared understanding of the expectations of an assessment.[9] Here's how to facilitate a class-constructed rubric.

First, split the class into the number of groups that aligns with the number of success criteria you plan to include on your writing rubric. If you have four success criteria, you would have four groups. You can assign success criteria to each group or allow each group to select the criterion they want to work with.

Once each group has its success criterion, they will work collaboratively using a blank rubric template, like the one pictured in Figure 4.1, to describe what their criterion looks like at each level of mastery: (1) beginning, (2) developing, (3) proficient, and (4) mastery. To do this, students must think critically about the skill or element of writing, engage in a conversation with the other members about this skill or element's essential attributes, and work collaboratively to craft descriptions of what the skill or element looks like at each level of mastery. This is a cognitively challenging task, but it demystifies the assessment process, making it clear what students are working toward as they write. You can have each group document their work on paper or in a collaborative online space, like Google Slides.

Figure 4.1: Student-Designed Rubric Using Success Criteria

Beginning 1	Developing 2	Proficient 3	Mastery 4

Teachers can facilitate a share-out followed by a carousel feedback activity where groups have the opportunity to share their work and receive feedback on their descriptions of each level of mastery. Teachers can give each group three to five minutes to present their success criteria and share their descriptions, explaining their thinking to the class. Then we recommend teachers give students time to provide feedback on the other groups' rubrics. They can physically carousel around the room using Post-it notes to leave comments with compliments, questions, and/or suggestions for each group, or, if they completed their work online, they can provide feedback in comments attached to the digital document or slide deck. Ultimately, we want students to think critically about each success criterion and how it is described at each level of mastery before we add it to a class rubric.

After this round of feedback, each group should reconvene to make the edits necessary to ensure their item on the class rubric is clear and student-friendly. Then the teacher can compile each group's element of the rubric into a larger class rubric for the writing assignment.

AI-Enhanced Strategy: AI-Generated Writing Samples for Students to Evaluate, Critique, and Discuss

Asking students to analyze and critique strong examples of writing can help them understand the elements of effective writing, such as structure, voice, and style, and provide them with a model of what they are working toward in their writing. Unless a teacher has kept samples of exemplary work created by previous students, generating strong examples for students to work with can be time-consuming.

We remember saving student work that knocked our socks off to use with future classes. Finding a strong student-generated example of an assignment was like gold! The problem is that a) we had to be organized enough to keep them, b) student exemplars are sometimes few and far between, and c) it meant we might be less likely to deviate from that prompt or assignment because we wanted to be able to show students what a strong example looked like.

Teachers can leverage AI technology to produce strong writing samples for students to analyze and critique, saving them significant time. Once teachers have generated two or three strong examples, they can structure the analysis process with an activity, like the analyzing writing exemplars activity pictured in Figure 4.2.

Figure 4.2: Analyzing Writing Exemplars

Analyzing Exemplars		
Exemplars	**Essential Elements** What elements do you notice in this exemplar?	**Strengths** What do you think is strong about this piece?
Exemplar #1		
Exemplar #2		
Exemplar #3		

Reflection	
What do all three exemplars have in common?	
What did you learn about analyzing these exemplars that you believe will help you to be successful on this assignment, task, or project?	
What questions do you have about this assignment, task, or project?	

To make this process engaging and collaborative in the classroom, teachers can strategically pair or group students for this exercise. This activity can be pulled into a station rotation lesson or built into a writing playlist.

By working together, students can share their perspectives and insights and learn from each other. Finally, teachers can ask students to apply what they have learned to their own writing, encouraging them to use strong examples as models for their work.

Wrap-Up

It is critical that students have a clear understanding of what success looks like as they plan disciplinary writing responses, and teachers can leverage numerous strategies to support this process. In addition to working with students to curate multiple exemplars, it is also valuable to scaffold how to deconstruct and analyze these exemplars to locate key elements and attributes. This empowers students to identify their own success criteria, which can be documented in a simple self-assessment rubric that students can use to guide them through the writing process. As we have shared throughout this chapter, here are the strategies you can use to support students in developing their disciplinary writing skills.

- Strategy #1: Use Exemplars from a Variety of Sources
- Strategy #2: Identify Key Attributes or Essential Elements
- Strategy #3: Embrace Non-examples, Too
- Strategy #4: Create a Simple Rubric
- AI-Enhanced Strategy: AI-Generated Writing Samples for Students to Evaluate, Critique, and Discuss

Reflect/Discuss

1. Consider how often you give students examples and models for disciplinary writing assessments. Which strategies do you use already? AI-generated examples? Work by former students? Your own work? Authentic examples from your field? How could you shift your process to provide additional examples for students to explore?
2. What is the value of providing explicit instruction in text types, structures, and attributes as you empower students to deconstruct and analyze texts?
3. How can analyzing texts help students co-create success criteria and a rubric for their own writing?

Putting It into Practice

The following playlist can be used to scaffold the strategies outlined in this chapter. Consider using or adapting with your students as you deconstruct and analyze exemplars.

Playlist: Create Your Own Success Criteria

Directions	Your Work
Reflection: Why is it valuable to analyze writing exemplars and non-examples before you begin to plan your own writing?	[Insert your text or a link]
Writing prompt: [insert writing prompt here] In your own words, what is your task, purpose, and audience for this writing prompt?	[Insert your text or a link]
Explore the two writing samples provided. As you explore each piece of writing, determine the author's tasks, purpose, and audience. Example: Non-example:	Notes on Model #1 Example: [Insert your text or a link] Notes on Model #2 Non-example: [Insert your text or a link]

Deconstructing and Analyzing Writing Samples

Discuss: With a partner, as part of a small group, or online in a discussion forum, share what you learned with your peers. What do the examples have in common? What is different about the examples? After engaging in a discussion, reflect on what you learned from the models.	[Insert your text, image, or a link]
Create: With a partner or as part of a small group, identify three success criteria you want to focus on as you design your rubric. Work collaboratively to discuss and then describe what the success criteria will look like at each level of mastery.	Success Criteria for _____ | 1 Beginning	2 Developing	3 Proficient	4 Mastery | |---|---|---|---| | | | | | | | | | | | | | | |
Reflection: What did you learn from this exercise? How do you think this process will impact how you plan for the writing prompt?	

5

Pre-writing and Planning

Flying by the Seat of My Pants

Katie My husband, Lon, and I love to play a game we invented called Restaurant Roulette. If you're ever on a date night or a road trip and you're hungry, you may want to give it a try. The rules are pretty simple. You are driving along when suddenly your stomach starts to growl. You realize you are starving and you need to stop to get something to eat. In most cases, there will be numerous options. You could start scrolling through reviews on Yelp to find the perfect place to eat; you could swing by a gas station and grab a bag of Combos, Bugles, or some gummy worms. Heck, you could just wait until you arrive at your destination and show your stomach who is boss. Lon and I don't love any of those options, so we made up Restaurant Roulette.

When you're en route and ready to eat, start looking for crowded areas. When you see an area that is fairly populated, pick a number from one to twenty, pull off the exit, and count off the restaurants as you drive along. When you identify the restaurant that corresponds to your number, you have to eat there. Easy peasy. So, let's say you

Pre-writing and Planning

choose the number sixteen. As you get off the exit, you look ahead, and you start to see some familiar signs: the usuals, like McDonald's and Olive Garden, as well as cozy diners and family restaurants tucked into strip malls. As you pass McDonald's, you yell out, "One," knowing that the Big Mac and chocolate shake are not in your near future.

The most important rule of the game is that you MUST eat at the restaurant where the number lands. We have been both pleasantly surprised and burned by this game. We had the best gyro we have ever had at a small diner in a strip mall, and we also forced ourselves into a Chinese food restaurant that smelled a little like hamster pee. In this case, we took our food to go. Refuse to eat at the "winning" restaurant? No way—that would ruin the integrity of the game.

We have brainwashed our kids to think this is a fun game as well. Road trips are endless rounds of Restaurant Roulette, usually with the kids leaning out the windows, watching fast-food restaurants go by, like high rollers at a real roulette table. Instead of, "C'mon, red . . ." It's "Come on, Dairy Queen." Cheers and disappointment are all a part of the fun.

Now, of course, you have to be flexible. If you're in a rural or remote area, you may have to choose a lower number or just get what you get and not get upset. While traveling to Stanley, Idaho, we adapted the game to "We are going to stop at the next place we see that serves food." It led us to pull over at a lovely "diner" that was someone's kitchen. We sat as the owner of the home made us breakfast sandwiches and served us coffee. When we asked what we owed, we were told whatever we could afford. Magical.

Many of you are likely horrified by our lack of planning and our spontaneity. My mother shares your pain. She has always said I am most comfortable flying by the seat of my pants.

When drafting this chapter, I decided to look up the meaning of that phrase. Someone who flies by the seat of their pants decides on a course of action as they go along, using their own initiative and perceptions rather than a predetermined plan. Yep, in many areas of my life, that's me. But when writing, no way. To fly by the seat of your pants when writing is a surefire way to crash the proverbial writing plane. And believe me, there is a lot of research that supports this.

Research and Reality

Pre-writing and planning are critical to the process of writing. Research is clear that it is common fact that writing is a recursive process in which students plan what to write, write down their ideas, and review what they have written.[1] Too often, educators place little emphasis on teaching students how to carry out critical planning for their writing.[2] As with all content and skills, students need explicit instruction in pre-writing and planning, as well as exemplars, scaffolds, and feedback. When teachers don't make this process visible, some students believe that they simply don't have ideas worth exploring. This is not true. Writing is a process—not an event.

The first stage of the writing process, pre-writing, prepares students to write by giving them an opportunity to reflect on the writing prompt; identify the task, purpose, and audience; brainstorm tentative ideas; and gather information for writing. During planning, students build on the pre-writing stage and think about how to organize their ideas to address the prompt. Students who have opportunities to pre-write and plan their writing perform significantly better than those who do not.[3]

Pre-writing Activities

Often teachers provide a prompt and expect students to generate a response, which can create significant anxiety or writer's block. This can be minimized, however, through pre-writing activities such as researching and taking notes, brainstorming, and freewriting and planning activities like using graphic organizers and outlining.

Researching and taking notes. Once students review a writing prompt, provide time for them to review resources to build background knowledge, activate their thinking, and allow them to begin jotting down notes that could inspire the planning process. Exploration of resources or research supports all writing prompts. For example, grade 3 students taking a standardized test in Massachusetts were given the following prompt: Based on *A Grand Old Tree* and *How the Forest Grew*, write a paragraph that explains how trees are important to animals. Support your response with important details from the story and the passage.

In this scenario, it is clear that students would read two passages to help them prepare for writing. Exploring resources before writing a response to a text ensures that students have the appropriate background knowledge to write about their topic, in this case, how trees are important to animals. Similarly, in high school chemistry, students may be given the prompt "Identify the shape of the formaldehyde molecule predicted by valence-shell electron-pair repulsion (VSEPR) theory. Explain your answer." These students would have a much better chance to write a quality response if they could first review a text that outlines VSEPR.

In these scenarios, researching and reviewing texts may seem like an obvious pre-writing activity, but providing such opportunities for students to build background knowledge before they write is valuable no matter the content area. For example, in an art class, a teacher may ask students, "Describe your favorite art project from this school year. Why was it your favorite?" Those students would be much better prepared to plan their writing if they had ten minutes to review the contents of their art portfolio before brainstorming.

Brainstorming is the idea-generating pre-writing strategy where students jot down whatever comes to mind as they think about a writing prompt. Brainstorming may include words, images, questions, and bullet points. If students sketch, draw, and use visuals to make connections, in combination with words or not, it is called depicting. The final brainstorm is a visual presentation that serves as a "container of ideas."[4] Concept maps, mind maps, and doodling are all examples of a depiction that may be used during brainstorming.

When students can explore resources first, brainstorming will likely be more fruitful. To support student brainstorming through the lens of UDL, you can provide options to work alone or with a partner, and to record ideas on chart paper, dry-erase boards, in writing notebooks, or using digital tools. If students struggle with this stage, it may be beneficial to use a station rotation to model brainstorming with small groups.

Collaborative brainstorming holds significant value, particularly for multilingual learners and students with disabilities. A recent study examined the differences in outcomes for multilingual students who completed individual pre-writing activities, like brainstorming, versus those who completed activities collaboratively. The learners who collaborated significantly outperformed the individual group on text length, some lexical and syntactic complexity measures, and all rating scores.[5]

Focused freewriting is a technique where learners write in response to a prompt (as opposed to traditional freewriting without a prompt) as quickly and continuously as possible. By writing without worrying about grammar, spelling, or punctuation, they are able to focus on generating ideas and thoughts related to the prompt. This can prevent writer's block and encourage more creative and fluid writing. A critical component of focused freewriting is reflection. After students freewrite for five to ten minutes, ask them to reflect on their writing and exclude irrelevant ideas that would not support the prompt.[6]

A cousin of focused freewriting is passage-based focused freewriting (PBFF), which asks students to read a passage and write freely on its key points, again, not worrying about editing. This technique combines review of resources and brainstorming in a single instructional activity.

Planning Activities

After pre-writing, students need to plan their writing. Planning is critical for students who may not know how to organize their ideas. Common planning strategies include completing graphic organizers, drafting outlines, and reviewing writing rubrics.

Graphic organizers are visual, graphic displays depicting relationships between ideas within a topic. This helps keep students on task while drafting, and graphic organizers have been shown to be effective in supporting students with learning disabilities in elementary, middle, and high schools in all content areas.[7] Unfortunately, they are not often used to prepare students to write. In a recent study, researchers found that graphic organizers were used to support student writing only 22 percent of the time in science and 37 percent of the time in social studies.[8] This provides an incredible opportunity to increase planning support across the content areas.

Outlining is another strategy to support planning, and some students may prefer it to completing a graphic organizer. When students create outlines, they identify topics and subtopics they want to write about before drafting their text. They then use this outline to guide their writing. Purdue's Online Writing Lab (OWL), one of the most frequently cited resources for writing, with close to 250 million visits a year, provides a quick and easy strategy to support student outlines. We love how the process begins with pre-writing activities that ask writers to first reflect on the task, purpose, and audience before completing an outline:

- Determine the purpose of your paper.
- Determine the audience you are writing for.
- Develop the thesis of your paper.

The next steps help writers craft the outline. Note how the process includes continued pre-writing:

- Brainstorm: List all the ideas that you want to include in your paper.
- Organize: Group related ideas together.
- Order: Arrange material in subsections from general to specific or from abstract to concrete.
- Label: Create main and sub headings.[9]

Although students can create outlines in many ways, two main types of outlines are the topic outline and the sentence outline. In the topic outline, the headings are given as single words or brief phrases. In the sentence outline, headings are expressed in complete sentences. When we planned this book, we used a combination of topic and sentence outlines, and having this outline was instrumental in our writing process! First, after brainstorming the need for such a book through late-night text exchanges, we created a tentative list of chapters and bullet points about what we wanted to cover in each. The original outline for our introduction looked like this:

- Tell the story of hearing about ChatGPT for the first time and our initial reactions
    - It might be fun to have both Catlin and Katie write about their initial reactions and compare/contrast them
- Just as COVID rocked education, disruptive technologies like ChatGPT threaten to do the same if we don't change our approach
    - ChatGPT is just the beginning

- Establish the value of writing across the curriculum
- Discuss why we wrote this book
- Note who the book is for
- Identify how the book is organized before providing a short wrap-up

Reviewing the writing rubric is another strategy to support planning. In the study mentioned above that examined the use of graphic organizers, writing rubrics were used even less frequently: 5 percent in science; 15 percent in social studies. Sharing writing expectations with students in a simple rubric is an important planning strategy because it provides students with a clear understanding of what is expected of them and how their work will be assessed. This helps to ensure that students stay focused and on-task throughout the writing process. When combined with other planning strategies like using graphic organizers or outlining, students are able to organize their ideas and plan their project more effectively, leading to much stronger writing aligned to task, purpose, and audience.

Strategy #1: Provide Options for Pre-writing

The writing process begins with pre-writing. When students engage in disciplinary writing activities, provide time for pre-writing activities. As with all strategies, there is no one-size-fits-all approach to pre-writing. We advise creating a choice board for pre-writing activities where students have options to activate their background knowledge and make their thinking visible before they start planning.

Pre-writing activities can be used in all content areas. In a career and technical education program, writing is often problem-based. According to career educator Patricia Hilliard, it is critical that all Career Technical Education (CTE) students know how to evaluate a problem, devise a solution, and present evidence to support the solution: "Whether that means presenting safety-gear recommendations for a construction site or a new marketing campaign to revitalize an old brand, it is important for students to know how to articulate their ideas in a logical, clear manner."[10]

As an example, Derek Martel, a high-performance automotive instructor at the New England Institute of Technology (NEIT), indicates in the course syllabus that students will be expected to produce writing.[11] When we asked about his writing prompts, he said he commonly shares case' studies that ask students to think critically and communicate their thoughts in writing because, in the field of automotive technology, mechanics have to document their process for repair orders. An example prompt may be "If a car has a check engine light and it has a particular trouble code associated with it, and the customer reported these symptoms, what would be your specific plan to diagnose the problem?"

Martel recognizes the importance of supporting students in the pre-writing and planning process. Students have options to participate in a discussion with classmates, schedule a one-on-one conversation with him, or review course materials, including technical manuals, videos, etc. to build background knowledge before they write. Martel notes that these pre-writing activities are critical because "you can usually tell that the student knows what they want to write, but they just don't know how to communicate it in writing, and that is when I would talk to them one-on-one and not put them in front of the class so they don't feel 'outed.'"

Using UDL and blended learning, you may use or adapt the following choice board (Table 5.1), so learners can choose meaningful pre-writing activities that can support them as they transition to the planning process. You can access a template for this choice board using the QR code at the beginning of this book.

Table 5.1: Pre-writing Choice Board

Pre-writing Choice Board	
Directions: After reviewing the writing prompt, choose one or more of the pre-writing activities below to activate background knowledge. You will have the option to collaborate and share the results of your pre-writing process with a partner or in a small group.	
Explore Resources to Activate Thinking • Something to read • Something to listen to • Something to watch	**Brainstorm** Dump whatever is in your brain onto paper or a digital file. Draw pictures, doodle, or use words and phrases.
Focused freewrite Put on a timer for five minutes. Using your notebook or digital tools, write everything you can think of in relationship to the writing prompt. Don't self-edit or pause to correct your thoughts.	**Instructor Chat** Come and have a one-on-one chat with me to share what you'd like to write about to get your juices flowing!

Strategy #2: STOP and LIST

Once students have completed the pre-writing stage and shared their results, building further background knowledge and fostering community, provide scaffold support so students can begin to plan their writing. This suggestion uses a specific evidence-based strategy called STOP and LIST to support students during the pre-writing/planning stages.[12] After reflecting on the writing prompt, ask students to "**S**top, **T**hink **O**f **P**urpose and **L**ist **I**deas, **S**equence **T**hem." You can use a simple graphic organizer that students can access in hard copy or digitally. This is also a great strategy to use on more standardized writing assignments. For this example, we chose a fifth-grade writing prompt from the SmarterBalanced, a standardized test that releases some items. After students read several sources about whales, they respond to the following prompt.

> Your class is making a storybook about adventures in the ocean to finish your Oceans Around the World unit. You will write a story to contribute to the class storybook. You have decided to write a story about a family that goes on vacation to a place right by the ocean. They go out on a boat ride and spot a huge creature coming out of the water. It's a whale! Tell the story of what happens when the family sees the whale.
>
> Your story will be read by your teacher and the other students in your class. When writing your story, find ways to use information and details from the sources to improve your story. Make sure you develop your character(s), the setting, and the plot, using details, dialogue, and description.

We asked Katie's son, Boden, who's seven, to read the excerpts about whales as a pre-writing activity and then asked him to plan using the graphic organizer. With very little support, he could use STOP and LIST. See his response in Table 5.2.

Table 5.2: STOP and LIST with Student Response

	Boden's Response
Stop, **T**hink **O**f **P**urpose (What is your task and purpose?)	A story about a family that went on a boat and saw a whale in the ocean
List Ideas	• Don't jump into the water • The whale shoots water at the family • They take a picture to keep • The whale has babies • And we would be on a big boat • We were in Nantucket
Sequence **T**hem (put them in order)	• We were in Nantucket • We went on a big boat • The whale shoots water at the family • The whale has babies • They take a picture to keep

Strategy #3: Provide Feedback on Planning Artifacts

Before students start drafting, provide feedback on their pre-writing and planning artifacts to ensure they are truly prepared for a successful writing experience. If student brainstorming or planning has led them down a path that doesn't align with writing prompts or expectations, we can address that early on to set students up for a much more successful experience.

You can use the station rotation model to support the reflection process. An online station can provide access to assignment rubrics, writing checklists, and exemplars for students to review. For example, you may create a choice board like the one in Table 5.3 so students have opportunities to reflect on all the resources they can use to monitor their progress as they engage in the drafting process.

In an offline station, students can share their pre-writing process with peers and provide feedback using a peer-feedback choice board (Table 5.4). (More on peer review in chapter 8.)

The last rotation gives small groups of students the opportunity to have a writing conference with you to receive targeted feedback and support for their planning process. You can review outlines and graphic organizers and support student goal-setting for the next steps in the writing process. The win-win is that students get more feedback about their pre-writing and planning, and the side-by-side assessment lets you avoid taking home the outlines and spending hours writing notes in the margins.

Table 5.3. Online Station Choice Board

Online Station Choice Board		
Online Station Directions: Choose at least one of the following resources to support your writing process. As you explore, be prepared to complete a digital exit ticket where you identify which resource(s) you selected and how those resources will support you in monitoring your progress as you draft your writing.		
 Review the Assignment Rubric	 Explore exemplars of high-quality writing to get inspired	 Review this writing process checklist

Table 5.4. Peer-Feedback Choice Board

Peer-Feedback Choice Board		
Directions: After sharing your pre-writing artifacts with peers, choose one of the following prompts to drive a conversation.		
Making Connections	**Tiny Tweaks**	**Celebrate Surprises**
As you reviewed the pre-writing artifact, what was similar about your pre-writing artifacts or process? What was different? Do you have suggestions for your peer to improve their work, or will this process drive you to make adjustments to your own work?	Identify one aspect of the pre-writing artifact that would benefit from a minor adjustment, modification, or tweak. What would you suggest the student rework so they are prepared for the planning and drafting stage?	As you reviewed this artifact, what surprised you about your peer's process? Was there an unexpected, original, outside-of-the-box, engaging, or particularly thought-provoking aspect to their pre-writing process? Describe how reviewing their pre-writing may impact your own process.

AI-Enhanced Strategy: Avoid Writer's Block with an AI Thought Partner

For many students, the most challenging part of the writing process is getting started. Students may be afraid of starting because they worry that their writing will not be good enough. This fear can be paralyzing and prevent them from even beginning. Other students may feel like everything they write needs to be perfect from the start. They may be overly critical of themselves and their writing, causing them to procrastinate. Regardless of the reason, for many students, writing those first few lines is the most daunting part. AI technology can be a helpful brainstorming partner, resource curator, and idea organizer!

A tool like ChatGPT can combat the paralysis that often accompanies a blank page or screen and help students generate ideas for their writing assignments by providing topic suggestions and a list of related keywords to help students develop and organize their thoughts on a topic. AI tools can also assist students in organizing their ideas into an outline by identifying key points, suggesting subtopics, and providing direction on the best way to present those ideas.

AI-powered search engines can help guide students during their research process. These tools can recommend relevant and credible sources, helping students navigate the vast amount of information on the internet.

By leveraging AI technology during the pre-writing process, students can benefit from efficient and effective support, allowing them to produce higher-quality writing in a shorter amount of time. Ultimately, this can lead to improved writing skills and increased confidence in their writing abilities.

Wrap-Up

Pre-writing and planning are critical steps in the writing process that are often overlooked. If we want all learners to learn to write, and write to learn, we have to provide them with explicit instruction in pre-writing and planning and offer numerous opportunities and choices for them to engage in each stage of the process, with feedback. Leveraging UDL and blended learning as students engage in pre-writing and planning can significantly improve student outcomes in writing and learning. Specific strategies outlined in this chapter include:

- Strategy #1: Provide Options for Pre-writing
- Strategy #2: STOP and LIST
- Strategy #3: Provide Feedback on Planning Artifacts
- AI-Enhanced Strategy: Avoid Writer's Block with an AI Thought Partner

Pre-writing and Planning

Reflect/Discuss

1. Do you provide explicit instruction, exemplars, and scaffolding of the pre-writing process? If so, how do your current practices align with the strategies in this chapter? If you don't yet, what practices can you put into place?
2. Do you provide explicit instruction, exemplars, and scaffolding of the planning process? If so, how do your current practices align with the strategies in this chapter? If you don't yet, what practices can you put into place?
3. How do UDL and blended learning make the pre-writing and planning process more self-directed and engaging for students?

Putting It into Action

Create a station rotation model that supports student pre-writing and planning and provides an opportunity for students to get feedback about their pre-writing and planning process. The following template can support you in your planning process.

	Teacher-led Station	**Online Station**	**Offline Station**
Pre-writing **Day 1**	Unpack the writing prompt to ensure understanding.	Students access digital choice board to support their pre-writing process.	Students choose to brainstorm or participate in focused freewriting to share initial ideas.
Planning **Day 2**	Students begin to plan their writing using graphic organizers or outlines.	Students access the assignment rubric and exemplars to support their planning process.	Peer review on pre-writing artifacts.
Your Ideas			

6

Writing in Class with Teacher Support and Feedback

Turns out I'm a Terrible Driver

Catlin My daughter turns sixteen this year and is learning to drive. I am equally excited and terrified to have my child behind the wheel of a car. Part of me cannot wait until she can drive herself to and from school, soccer, appointments, and friends' houses. For the last five years, I have felt a bit like an Uber driver. I blame competitive soccer; it's the primary culprit. My kids play on club teams that practice in the afternoons, often in different locations and at different times, so it is not unusual for me to leave work at 2:00 p.m. and not get home until after 7:00 p.m.

So, with excitement and a fair bit of dread, I helped Cheyenne sign up for her driver's education classes. She opted to take her courses online instead of losing three Saturdays to in-person classes. I couldn't blame her. As she progressed through the twenty online modules, she would chat my ear off about what she was learning. She would quiz me: "Hey, Mom, do you know how much the fine is for leaving an animal in your car?" "Mom, did you know that you are supposed to have one car length for every ten miles per hour when driving on the freeway?" "Mom, do you know which direction to turn your wheels if you are parking uphill?" I'm pretty sure Cheyenne left most of our conversations convinced that I should not have a license.

She also became a critical observer in the passenger seat! I have been driving this child around her whole life, but now she saw my driving through new eyes. "Mom, you're going ten miles over the speed limit!" "Mom, you didn't use your blinker." "Mom, you need to come to a complete stop." Ugh. I've had to shelve some of the bad driving habits I've cultivated over the years. So, now we leave the house early, and I take lots of deep breaths in the car to ensure we get to our destination on time and in line with California's traffic laws.

As Cheyenne neared the end of her twenty modules, she began to express concern that she was learning a lot about the rules but not *how* to drive: "Mom, there is so much information about what a person can and cannot do and a bunch of technical details about how to drive, but I don't feel like I am prepared to drive. I thought I would feel more prepared after this course." I explained that, like anything else, there's no substitute for practice. She won't feel confident driving until she has done it for a while. I told her the best way to learn would be to drive with me and be receptive to my suggestions and feedback as she drives.

Sure enough, her confidence grew as she spent time behind the wheel with me in the passenger seat. She asked a million questions. We talked the whole time. I complimented her when she made a smart choice, offered suggestions when she was frustrated or flustered, and highlighted things other drivers were doing that I thought might help her. The experience was not entirely smooth. There were moments of extreme stress when she was exasperated because I slammed my foot down on an imaginary brake. She shed a few tears after a particularly scary merge onto a crowded freeway. Despite the bumps, her time behind the wheel practicing with support is what ultimately will give her the confidence to drive alone.

Writing, much like driving, is a cognitively complex task that integrates many skills, including writing mechanics, comprehension of content, awareness of the audience, and understanding of structure and purpose. To become good writers, students need dedicated class time to practice and regular feedback on their writing. Feedback is key to helping students, and teenage drivers, learn what they are doing well and what they need to work on.

Research and Reality

Feedback is how students feel seen and supported as they learn. Unfortunately, feedback is easy to neglect in a classroom where teachers feel pressure to cover the curriculum, with significant time spent transferring information, unpacking complex concepts, and modeling strategies and skills. We know this coverage mentality is driven by pressure to keep up with rigid pacing guides and prepare students for standardized exams, but it creates an alarming imbalance in classrooms.[1] The time we spend explaining how to do something—apply a strategy, execute a skill, or compose a piece of writing—should be balanced with the time we spend giving students specific, actionable feedback as they practice. We can talk all day about *how* students should do something. But it's when students attempt to take what they learned from a mini-lesson or lecture and apply it that they are likely to hit bumps, have questions, and need support.[2] That's where feedback is critical.

In addition to the imbalance between instruction and feedback in classrooms, the "feedback" that is typically provided isn't actually feedback. Comments like "Well done," "This is incorrect," or a grade or point value, like C+ or 8/10, do not provide insight into what was specifically done well and what needs to be developed or revised and are unlikely to move students toward a specific writing target. That may be, in part, why students often do not use the feedback they receive to modify their work and, as a result, why this feedback does not result in learning as it is intended.[3] If feedback is going to drive deeper learning and significantly impact student achievement, students must understand it and use it to improve their work.

Grant Wiggins, co-creator of the Understanding by Design (UbD) framework, defined feedback as "information about how we are doing in our efforts to reach a goal" and identified some characteristics of effective feedback:

- goal-oriented
- transparent and clear
- actionable
- focused and specific
- timely[4]

Let's explore these characteristics to see how we can integrate them into our feedback to ensure it is a powerful tool for improvement and growth in the classroom.

Goal-Oriented

Knowing your destination is key to understanding if you are on the right track or are lost and need directions. Similarly, for feedback to be effective, students need to have a clear understanding of the expectations and standards.[5] Are they writing an argumentative piece to persuade their reader to agree with a particular perspective on an issue? Are they writing stories rich with descriptive language and dynamic characters to entertain their audience? Are they describing a process in detail so the reader can replicate it? Instead of simply writing praise or correcting mechanical errors, articulating a clear goal makes giving focused feedback easier for us as teachers, while also making feedback easier for students to understand because they know where they are heading and have the guidance to make the necessary adjustments to get there.

Teachers can help students to identify the goal or objective of a particular writing assignment by providing a clear, standards-aligned rubric at the start of any writing assignment that will be assessed. Rubrics, like the one pictured in Figure 6.1, provide a roadmap for the writing destination students are moving toward. (We'll chat more about standard-aligned rubrics in chapter 10.)

Once students have the rubric, encourage them to use it to identify a goal they have for themselves. Each student will have different elements of the writing process they want and need to develop and improve on, and setting a goal for themselves at the beginning of an assignment will encourage them to think about what those elements are for them. Some students may be in the beginning stages of writing an opinion statement with clear reasons while others may want to focus on developing their explanations with strong details and accurate information.

When asking students to set a goal for themselves, it is helpful to provide a structure they can use to articulate their goal and think about what they will need to do to achieve it. For example, the graphic organizer pictured in Figure 6.2 walks students through a three-part goal-setting process.

First, students must decide what their goal is for a specific writing assignment. What is their destination? What do they hope to accomplish in their writing? The second section asks them to think about how they will progress toward that goal. What actions and behaviors will take them closer to their destination? Finally, they are encouraged to think about what it will look or feel like to achieve their goal. Completing this goal-setting process on paper, digitally, or in a video recording at the beginning of a writing assignment can help students frame and focus their energy and efforts as they write. It also provides teachers with a lens to look at student work so they can give targeted feedback on this area of focus.

Writing in Class with Teacher Support and Feedback

Students need opportunities to think about their learning in intentional ways, and structured goal setting is a powerful way to cultivate expert learners who understand their strengths, limitations, and areas where they need additional support.

Figure 6.1: Elementary Opinion Writing Rubric

Criteria	Beginning 1	Developing 2	Proficient 3	Mastery 4
Opinion with Reasons	Opinion is unclear; no reasons are given.	Opinion is clear but reasons are unclear or incomplete.	Opinion is clearly stated and reasons are stated.	Opinion is clearly stated and reasons are strong.
Evidence	Opinion is not supported. No evidence (e.g., facts, examples) is provided.	Attempts to support opinion and reasons with facts; however, the information is unclear or inaccurate.	Supports opinion and reasons with facts and necessary details.	Supports opinion and reasons with strong, accurate facts and thorough details.
Explanation	Little to no explanation of the information presented.	Explanation attempts to discuss the information but is unclear at times.	Clear explanation that discusses most of the information presented.	Clear and concise explanation that thoroughly discusses the information presented.

Figure 6.2: Goal-Setting Graphic Organizer

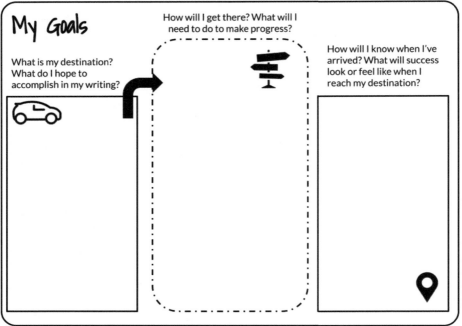

Transparent and Clear

Once teachers have established a clear goal, Wiggins's UbD guidelines say the feedback must be transparent and tangible. We've both had the experience of underlining sentences and writing "awk" (repeatedly, for years) on students' papers, only to eventually have a child say, "What does this mean?" It was disconcerting to face that question because we thought using the abbreviation for *awkward* to identify a sentence that didn't flow smoothly or communicate a clear idea would signal to a student that they needed to rework that sentence. However, that comment on a paper doesn't help students understand *why* the phrasing is awkward or *how* to go about reworking the sentence to flow more cogently. Feedback that's opaque or unclear to students is not going to help them improve or make progress toward their writing goals.

One way to ensure transparency is to dedicate time to reviewing feedback in a small-group setting at the teacher-led station in a station rotation lesson. Especially at the beginning of the year, when teachers and students are getting to know one another, or when students are learning how to compose a new type of writing, making time to review and discuss feedback ensures students understand what the feedback means and what they should do with it. Teachers can guide students as they review their feedback, answer questions, clarify terms, and provide suggestions for how to act on their feedback. That way, feedback is a powerful tool for improvement instead of being opaque, unclear, and ineffective.

Actionable

Feedback should lead to action. Teachers want to avoid the "feedback gap," or the space between the promise and potential that feedback has to create positive change and growth and the actual use (or lack thereof) of the feedback.[6]

The best way to avoid the feedback gap is to 1) make sure that feedback is focused and specific and 2) require that students do something with their feedback.

Too often, feedback happens once a piece of writing has been submitted. It functions to validate or support the grade or point value assigned to the composition, instead of as a tool the writer can use to improve their work before it is assessed. When feedback is given on finished products that students are not required to revise and resubmit, it has very little impact on the quality of their writing or their understanding of themselves as writers.

On the other hand, formative feedback during the writing process is much more likely to help students develop and improve their writing. The Stanford Teaching Commons describes formative feedback as helping students recognize gaps in their knowledge, areas to improve, what support resources they may need, and learning strategies they might change or adapt to meet the course outcomes. Without formative feedback, students may not be aware of their own misunderstandings.[7] This can later lead to confusion and cause students to lose motivation.

Formative feedback can come as synchronous verbal comments, written comments, and audio or video recordings of students' works in progress. This helps students develop higher levels of self-efficacy as they work on writing assignments because they feel supported as they write.

Focused and Specific

Feedback also needs to be focused and specific if students are going to use it to revise, develop, or improve their writing. What specific elements are missing? What phrase or claim needs more support? What questions might they ask themselves to develop a line of reasoning or explanation? The more detailed and concrete the feedback, the more likely it is that students will know how to use it to improve their writing.

It's tempting to try to fix every mistake or error when providing students with feedback on their work in progress, but feedback on minutia can be hard for students to take in, process, and act on. Instead, teachers should adopt a "less is more" approach. Since we are going to make the case that feedback be a regular part of your class, you don't need to give it on every aspect of the assignment at once. When you have multiple opportunities to give feedback, we suggest you limit yourself to addressing one or two aspects of a student's writing. That way, they can review and act on the feedback without being overwhelmed by a document covered in corrections and comments.

Before a feedback session, we suggest you clearly identify the element(s) of the assignment you plan to focus on, so students know in advance you are not looking at every aspect of the assignment but rather a particular part. Using a form like the one pictured in Table 6.1 can keep your feedback focused while challenging students to read it, put it in their own words, and explain how they plan to act on it.

Table 6.1: Feedback Session Form

Feedback Session Form		
Focus element(s)	Feedback in your own words	What do you plan to do with it? Where to next?

Timely

Feedback on a complex process, like writing, is best when it is provided *as* students work. Unfortunately, traditional approaches to instruction are so time-consuming that teachers take student writing home to provide feedback during their evenings and weekends. Because teachers may have anywhere from 30–160 students, this creates a time lag. After teachers make all these comments and suggestions in isolation, students are left to review and process that information in isolation. There isn't the time and space for a conversation about students' progress or the feedback they receive.[8] That may make it challenging for students to act on the feedback to improve their writing.

A teacher's role as the instructor is a valuable aspect of their work; however, it can consume so much class time that teachers neglect their role as facilitators who support students as they work with formative feedback. We encourage teachers to find a better balance between the time they spend on instruction versus the time they spend giving timely feedback as students attempt to do something with that instruction. That's where the flipped classroom model is particularly useful in shifting some instruction and explanation online to free teachers from the front of the room. Since most formal writing assignments take more than one sitting to compose, as we suggest in chapter 3, teachers can lean on video instruction to transfer information they plan to present to everyone the same way so students can control the pace at which they consume and process that information. Teachers can then dedicate their time and attention to giving feedback at key moments during the writing process to identify areas of strength, gaps or areas in need of development, and misconceptions or inaccurate information. Students can immediately put suggestions and strategies into practice, or can ask for clarification if they do not understand the feedback or for support if they are unsure how to implement it.

Let's explore how teachers can use the station rotation or playlist model to pull feedback into the classroom where it belongs!

Strategy #1: The Station Rotation Model and Real-Time Feedback

The station rotation model moves students through a series of three types of "stations" or learning activities: teacher-led, online, and offline. The teacher-led station is perfect for providing students with feedback on their writing as they work; however, there will likely be anywhere from four to eight students at that station, depending on the size of the class and the total number of stations in use. That means teachers must be strategic about how they use their time and focus their feedback on one or two elements of the writing process. They will not be able to fix everything; instead, they can supplement their teacher feedback and position students to think critically about their writing, using peer feedback and technology tools, like Grammarly. (We chat more about these in chapters 8 and 9, respectively.)

Figure 6.3 shows an example of a writing-focused station rotation where the teacher-led station is dedicated to feedback. At the start of the teacher-led station, the teacher should clearly define the goal of that day's revision session and explicitly state the expectations for what students should do when they receive feedback to ensure the teacher's comments and suggestions lead to student action.

- What specific element of the student's writing will they provide feedback on?
- What should students do with the feedback they receive? Should they make the corrections and attempt a revision? Will they need to craft a "where to next" statement based on the feedback they received or complete a short reflection?
- What should students do if they have a question while they work? Should they write it on a Post-it note or add a comment to their digital document?

Figure 6.3: Writing-Focused Station Rotation

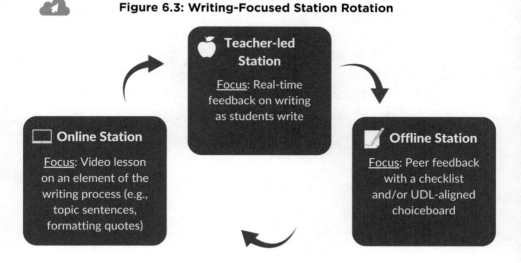

When teachers lead a small-group station focused on feedback, they may physically carousel around the table to give written feedback on offline work or jump into and out of digital documents, leaving comments, suggestions, questions, and links to writing videos that can support students in editing and revising. We encourage teachers to document the feedback in writing or audio recordings, since verbal feedback may be challenging for students to remember or understand.

Real-time feedback sessions have several benefits over traditional approaches. First, it builds time into the lesson for students to continue writing. Given the many things vying for their attention outside of school, students appreciate having dedicated time to work on a writing assignment in class. Second, because teachers will have limited time to spend with each student's writing, the feedback must be focused and specific. Third, if the feedback isn't clear and transparent to students, they can ask for clarification in the moment instead of trying to process it on their own. Finally, since a real-time feedback session should have a clear protocol for what students do with the feedback, students will be required to act on that feedback to improve their writing. Encourage students to consider three questions when it comes to feedback: Where am I going? How am I going there? Where to next?[9] These three questions drive metacognitive skill-building around the writing process and help students to understand themselves better as writers and learners. Table 6.2 includes tips for running a teacher-led feedback station.

Table 6.2: Tips for Running a Teacher-Led Feedback Station for Writing

Tips for Running a Teacher-Led Feedback Station for Writing	
Tip 1: Identify the element of writing you plan to give feedback on before the session.	As with all things in education, explaining the *why* or purpose of focusing on this element of their writing can help students appreciate the value of a real-time feedback station.
Tip 2: Decide how much time you will spend on each student's writing in advance.	Divide the number of students by the time you have with them at your station and use a timer to keep yourself on track.
Tip 3: Set up custom shortcuts for commonly used comments in your Google Doc or browser to save time.	When students work on a writing assignment, it is common for teachers to make the same comments on multiple papers. If you tend to use the same comments, ask the same questions, or provide the same link to a writing video on multiple digital documents, custom shortcuts can be a game changer, saving you significant time.
Tip 4: Provide an avenue for students to ask questions without interrupting your feedback flow.	Students are bound to have questions, but you don't want those to derail a feedback session. Instead, encourage students to write their questions on a colorful Post-it and put it at the top of their offline writing or add a digital comment to the top of their online document. That way, as you physically carousel around the group or dive into and out of digital documents giving feedback, you can address their questions.

Tip 5: Make it clear what students should do after receiving feedback.	It's key that students act on the feedback they receive. Tell them if they should revise their writing and use a highlighter (actual or digital) to show what they've added or changed. You can encourage a reflective practice about what they learned from the feedback and how it impacted their writing. You can also ask them to answer, "Where to next?" identifying what they need to do to continue improving their writing.

Strategy #2: Build Teacher Check-ins into the Playlist Model to Provide Feedback

The playlist model presents students with a sequence of learning activities designed to move them toward a clear learning objective or goal. The playlist model is ideal for any complex task or series of tasks that may benefit from students having variable time on task. Writing is the perfect example of a cognitively complex task that takes students different amounts of time to complete. Some students can draft a piece of writing in a single sitting with little support, while others need more time and support to plan, process, write, and revise a single piece. A writing playlist allows students to self-pace through a sequence of learning activities designed to help them compose a particular piece of writing.

Let's look at the excerpt from the document-based question (DBQ) writing playlist pictured in Figure 6.4. This DBQ playlist demonstrates how teachers can use a blended learning model that integrates the principles of UDL to give students more control over the pace of their learning while inviting them to make key decisions throughout the process. There are moments in the playlist when they can choose to work alone, with a partner, or as part of a group. They can decide how to capture notes and organize their ideas as they read through the documents.

Teachers may wonder how they can foster collaboration or allow students to work with a partner or group at particular moments in the playlist. We suggest using a public tracker system online (e.g., spreadsheet) or offline (e.g., moving magnets on a whiteboard to show the activity they're currently working on). That way, students can quickly identify other members of the class who are working on the same step of the playlist if they want to connect with another student to complete a task, like using a reciprocal reading strategy to read through the documents.

In addition to the individual learning activities in the "path" of the playlist, there are key moments when students are directed to pause for a "teacher check-in." In these moments, students need to take their work and meet with the teacher to receive feedback and discuss their progress. Teachers can select a specific element of the writing assignment to look at and give feedback, like the first draft of a thesis statement or body paragraph. Teachers will want to establish a clear protocol for what students should do following the check-in conversation. For example, in the DBQ playlist below, there is a spot for students to revise their thesis statements immediately following the teacher check-in.

These teacher check-ins also provide the time and space for students to ask questions or seek support if they are unsure about or struggling with some aspect of the writing assignment. Teachers can modify a student's playlist based on these conversations, adding additional resources and scaffolds or encouraging particular students to compare and discuss their work. These moments allow for a degree of differentiation and personalization that is likely to help students feel more confident as they navigate this assignment.

Figure 6.4: DBQ Writing Playlist

Document-Based Question Playlist

Path	Student Work
The Question • Individually or with a partner, read the question three times, highlight key words/phrases, and discuss what the question is asking you to prove.	Insert a clear statement about what the question is asking you to prove.
Analyzing Exemplars • Individually or with a partner, select two of the exemplars to analyze. • Identify three essential elements you think need to be included in your DBQ based on your review of these exemplars.	List essential DBQ elements: 1. 2. 3.
Deep Dive into Documents • Individually, with a partner, or as part of a small group using the reciprocal reading strategy, read and analyze the documents. • As you explore the documents, document your learning with one option from the choice board.	**Active Reading Choice Board** **Classic Annotations**: Do you love to make notes in the margins of your text as you read? Enjoy getting a little crazy with your highlighter? Feel free to engage with your book and send me some pictures! **Sketchnotes**: Are you artistic? Do you enjoy the tactile experience of drawing on paper, or do you like online graphics programs? Feel free to capture your notes visually with drawings and sketches! **Concept Map**: Like the simplicity of a concept map or flowchart? Organize concepts visually in a way that makes sense to you! Play with a hierarchical structure of concepts. Go nuts with arrows, golden lines, and questions!

Writing in Class with Teacher Support and Feedback

Video Instruction: Thesis Statement • Watch this video on how to write a thesis statement, then write your own. • Find a classmate to exchange thesis statements with for feedback.	Write your thesis statement below.

Teacher Check-in: Feedback on Thesis Statement

Thesis Statement Revision • Use the feedback you received during your check-in to revise your thesis statement.	Revised thesis statement.

Digging for Details • Complete the graphic organizer with your key points and find evidence from the documents to support those points.	*DBQ Planning Graphic Organizer* Thesis Statement: | Point #1: | Point #2: | Point #3: | | Evidence: • | Evidence: • | Evidence: • |

Video Instruction: Body Paragraph • Structure • Watch this video on how to structure your body paragraph, then write your own. • Find a classmate to exchange paragraphs with for feedback.	

Teacher Check-in: Feedback on Body Paragraph

Strategy #3: Giving Feedback to Students Working Online

Research indicates that using media, beyond text comments, improves students' perceptions of feedback quality. Online students who received audio feedback perceived that feedback as more thorough, detailed, and personal than text feedback.[10] Students also reported being more motivated by audio and video feedback because it was clear and personalized.[11] Interestingly, teachers also reported higher levels of engagement when giving video and audio feedback. Table 6.3 presents three strategies teachers working online can use to give students more focused, actionable, and personalized feedback.

Table 6.3: Three Feedback Strategies for Teachers Working with Students Online

Three Feedback Strategies for Teachers Working with Students Online	
Strategy #1: Host real-time feedback sessions using video conferencing software.	Teachers working exclusively online can adapt this real-time feedback strategy described earlier for the online environment with video conferencing software. If students are working on a writing assignment, teachers can schedule five-minute feedback sessions with individual students. During these real-time feedback sessions, teachers can provide students with feedback about their work. • Where do they see evidence of growth? • Which aspects of the work would benefit from further development? • Where are the gaps or missing elements?

Strategy #2: Record video comments with a screencasting tool.	Teachers may not be able to require their students to attend a live feedback session, or they may want to give students a choice between synchronous and asynchronous feedback. In that case, they can record a short screencast, giving students feedback on their work. Teachers can pull up the students' work on their computer screens, click the screen recording tool, select desktop recording, and record their feedback. As they provide feedback, they can highlight specific elements of a student's work, so the feedback is easier to follow. When the recording is finished, teachers can share the link to the recording directly with the student.
Strategy #3: Record audio comments.	Audio comments are another way to capture feedback on digital writing. Teachers can record a single audio note or attach individual notes to different parts of the writing assignment. Some audio comment tools provide a transcript in addition to the audio recording to increase accessibility. Others allow students to ask questions in response to an audio note to make the process of receiving feedback more interactive.

Feedback that feels personalized is more likely to inspire students to continue working to develop their writing skills. As teachers play with these strategies and leverage different types of media to provide feedback, it is important to remember that "less is more." Giving students a laundry list of items to work on is overwhelming. Instead, try to keep feedback focused on one or two elements of their work and make it clear how they can act on that feedback to improve their writing. The more focused and actionable the feedback, the more likely students are to use it.

You may also find that students have specific preferences about how they want to receive their feedback. To honor their learning preferences, teachers can ask students what type of feedback would be most comfortable and helpful, using a choice board like the one pictured in Figure 6.5.

Figure 6.5: Feedback Choice Board

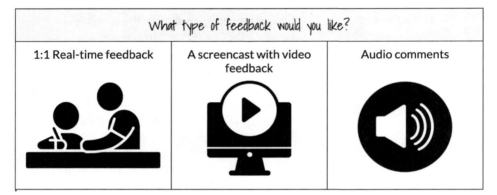

AI-Enhanced Strategy: A Virtual Tutor

Feedback is how students feel seen and supported in a classroom, but teachers are juggling a lot and may not have time to look at each student's work to provide meaningful feedback. AI technology, on the other hand, can give instant feedback anytime, anywhere. Students can receive feedback on their writing as soon as they finish, without waiting for their teacher. AI technology can serve as a personal tutor! This is more likely to be motivating since it eliminates the wait time between completing a task and getting feedback. Essentially, students can stay in the flow and engage in more self-directed work in the classroom (and beyond).

AI feedback is specific and targeted, helping students to identify areas for improvement in their writing, such as grammar, syntax, and organization. This type of feedback can help students develop their writing skills more effectively and efficiently, as they can receive guidance on areas of weakness in real-time and make improvements as they go.

Students can ask questions, like the ones listed below, to gather specific feedback on their writing assignments in progress.

- Can you check my grammar and punctuation in this paragraph?
- Does this sentence make sense?
- Can you suggest ways to improve the flow of my essay?
- Is my thesis statement clear and concise?
- Can you suggest alternative words or phrases to improve my writing?
- Do I have any run-on sentences or sentence fragments in my writing?
- Can you check if my citations are correct?
- Is my writing style appropriate for the audience and purpose of my writing?
- Can you provide feedback on the organization and structure of my essay?
- Can you check if I am using the correct verb tense throughout my writing?

AI feedback may also be more objective and unbiased than feedback from a teacher because it is based on data and algorithms rather than personal opinions. This can help ensure that all students receive consistent and equitable feedback, regardless of their background or performance. It also presents an opportunity for students to think critically about the feedback they receive, since algorithms may suggest edits or revisions that do not work to improve a piece.

Wrap-Up

Feedback often takes a back seat to instruction. Teachers spend significant time explaining the parts of the writing process, but not enough time sitting alongside learners coaching them and providing feedback as they write. We want teachers to use blended learning and UDL to shift writing and feedback on writing into the classroom, so students feel supported *as* they write.

The best feedback is given in relation to a goal, so we want to make the purpose of any writing assignment crystal clear to students. The most effective feedback is transparent, specific, actionable, and timely. Pulling feedback into our classes not only accomplishes these objectives, but it lightens the workload for teachers outside of class. Utilizing the following strategies can help you to make this shift:

- Strategy #1: The Station Rotation Model and Real-Time Feedback
- Strategy #2: Playlist: Use Teacher Check-ins to Provide Feedback
- Strategy #3: Giving Feedback to Students Working Online
- AI-Enhanced Strategy: A Virtual Tutor

Reflect/Discuss

1. When, where, and how often do you give feedback on student writing?
2. What is challenging about your current approach to giving feedback?
3. If you had to break up a pie chart into one wedge representing the amount of class time you dedicate to instruction and a second wedge representing the amount of time you dedicate to giving students feedback as they work, what would your pie chart look like? How might you strive for more balance in terms of the time you dedicate to instruction and feedback?
4. What impact would moving feedback into the classroom using blended learning models have on your workload?

5. What impact might giving feedback in real-time as students write have on your students' feelings about writing in your class?
6. What types of writing assignments do you typically ask students to complete for your class? How might you integrate feedback loops into these assignments?

Put It into Practice

- Select a complex writing assignment you plan to have students do this year. Think about the steps involved in completing this piece of writing. Select a blended learning model or models to use to shift the bulk of the writing into the classroom, where you can give students feedback as they write.
- Decide if you want to use the station rotation or playlist model to build time into your lessons for your feedback sessions. Design a series of station rotation lessons that free you to use your teacher-led station for real-time feedback, or create a playlist that allows students to self-pace through the process and meet with you at strategic moments in the playlist for one-on-one feedback sessions.
- Reflect on how you can ensure your feedback is goal-oriented, transparent and clear, actionable, focused and specific, and timely.

7

Writing Conferences and Personalized Support

Type-A Meets Dr. J

Catlin The people close to me have lovingly dubbed me "the honey badger" because of my type-A tendencies. I am a hard worker who has always been able to overcome life's challenges by sheer force of will, but that tendency to plow through life and resolve problems on my own came to a head at the end of 2019. That's when my doctoral journey shifted from attending regular in-person classes with my small, tight-knit cohort to preparing for my research study on blended learning. I returned home after those last few classes consumed by a deep sadness.

I had never experienced depression before, but I felt adrift for the first time in my adult life. I tried to deal with my complicated emotions using exercise. I literally tried to run away from my feelings. Whenever I felt overwhelmed and sad, I would lace up my tennis shoes and run the track. I ran until my body was exhausted, my legs trembling and my mind numb. I thought I could escape my feelings with physical exertion. I was wrong. After a long conversation with my best friend, I realized I needed to find a therapist to talk to.

I remember going to her office for the first time. The building was an old Victorian; its rooms had been converted into a collection of office suites for therapists. I sat in a hard wooden chair at the bottom of the stairs in the dark lobby, staring at the small dust particles floating in the rays of sunlight coming through the windows. There was a whoosh of sound machines playing white noise outside several doors to mask what I can only assume were very personal conversations. The place smelled like an old library. I found myself getting uncomfortable and shifting in my seat. I had a moment when I seriously considered leaving. Did I want to do this? Was I prepared to explore why I was feeling this way and talk to a stranger about personal parts of my life?

"Catlin, is that you?" The voice was kind and clear and belonged to a smiling face that appeared over the railing of the second floor. I took a deep breath. *Well, it's too late to make a run for it now.* I climbed the stairs, which creaked and groaned as I walked up them. It felt ominous.

Dr. J, my therapist, ushered me into a cozy little office with a big chair (hers), a worn two-seater couch (mine), and bright windows. Our initial conversation felt like a first date. She was getting to know me. She wanted to understand why I had sought out therapy. I explained that I had been feeling "off" but wasn't sure why. I told her a few friends had asked if I was OK. I hadn't had much of an appetite for weeks. And I was worried that my kids might notice I wasn't quite myself. I didn't want the people in my life worrying about me. I was used to powering my way through problems, so I wanted to figure out what was wrong and fix it.

I left feeling a little underwhelmed by that first visit, but I went back. In fact, I kept going back every week. Dr. J asked a lot of questions, and she listened . . . I mean *really* listened. Even though I had taught for years and was a public speaker, I had never had anyone's undivided attention or been anyone's sole focus the way I was in her office. Her questions and the conversations they sparked helped me to understand myself on a deep level. I discovered that my sadness was coming from a place of loss. It wasn't just that I was losing my cohort and the fulfillment of that need for community as I transitioned from classes where we were all together to my research study, which would be an individual endeavor. My feelings were compounded by my experience eighteen months prior when I had resigned from my teaching position after a wildfire destroyed my family's home and forced us to relocate to a new city. I had taught at Windsor High School for sixteen years and developed deep bonds with many of my colleagues. And if I wasn't a teacher, what was I? In a matter of months, I lost my home, my community, and my identity.

Just months before the fire, I had started my doctoral program and stubbornly refused to quit or take a leave of absence. Apparently, I shifted my desire for community and identity onto my new cohort and my work as a doctoral student. I threw myself into the experience. At the time, it was a great distraction from the fire and its aftermath. As I worked with Dr. J, considering her questions and answering them honestly, I understood my sadness and began to develop the tools to process those feelings in a healthy way. It wasn't until I actively engaged in the process of exploring my experiences and their impact on me that I began to truly understand myself.

Like my experience facing a situation I could not power through on my own, there are academic challenges that students will not be able to tackle alone. They will need personalized support and guidance to overcome these challenges. Students who have the opportunity to sit with a patient and caring professional—like I did with Dr. J, but in this case, with a teacher—who asks questions and listens attentively are likely to feel seen and supported and walk away from the experience with a deep awareness of themselves as writers and thinkers. That is the potential power of a writing conference.

Research and Reality

Writing conferences engage students in conversations about their work, encouraging them to take an active role in exploring their writing to understand their process and the content they are writing about on a much deeper level. These conversations create space for teachers to review student writing, identify areas of strength and areas that require development or revision, to provide individualized guidance and tips on improving specific aspects of the student's writing, such as organization, grammar, and style, and to discuss a student's progress. Having this one-on-one time and attention focused on their writing can help students feel more confident and empowered in their writing abilities and can positively impact the student's writing skills and higher-order and critical thinking skills.[1]

Writing conferences clarify the teacher's expectations for the assignment and help students better understand the objectives of a piece of writing. Following a conference, students can reflect on their writing process, the content of their writing, and the ways they can improve their writing.

In addition to improving writing skills, confidence, and independence, when teachers engage students in a writing conference with the goal of treating them as partners in the learning process, students gain agency and a voice. This allows them to become active participants—asking for clarification and advocating for their ideas—in a way that isn't possible when they receive written feedback alone. Conferencing helps us share the responsibility for learning with our students.

When teachers develop a regular practice of conferencing and approach conferences with patience and a desire to engage their students in meaningful discussions about writing, they also create opportunities to build positive relationships with learners.[2] This can lead to more productive and supportive learning experiences. During a writing conference, both the teacher and learners gain insight into the student's progress, which makes it possible for teachers to better meet their students' needs. Students begin to see their teachers as supportive partners in this work as they develop into expert learners and writers.[3]

Despite the myriad benefits of conferencing about students' writing, this is not a common practice in classrooms because it requires time. Teachers who rely on the whole-group, teacher-led approach to instruction do not have that time, which is another reason we advocate for teachers to use universally designed blended learning models to architect student-centered lessons that free them to do this important work. This shift from whole-group, teacher-led learning to small-group, student-centered learning requires a shift in approach to lesson design and intentional work to help students develop as self-directed learners, but the payoff is that teachers will be able to sit alongside students to support their individual progress.

The benefits of writing conferences extend far beyond the quality of writing itself and encourage students to think more deeply about the content they are writing about. So, even teachers who have not been trained on *how* to teach the skill of writing can use writing conferences to encourage deeper thinking about the concepts, questions, processes, issues, and phenomena at the heart of the writing assignment.

As shown in Table 7.1, research indicates that writing conferences are ineffective when they focus too heavily on mechanics and grammar, with the teacher dominating the experience as they identify problems and correct mistakes without student input. The most effective conferences include equitable discussions between the student and teacher about the content of a piece of writing and employ active listening, questioning, and collaboration to help students improve it.

Table 7.1: Effective Versus Ineffective Writing Conferences

Effective Writing Conferences	Ineffective Writing Conferences
• Include equitable discussions about the writing assignment in progress • Focus on identifying solutions for aspects of the writing assignment that need to be developed or reworked • Provide teacher and student equal time to share ideas, ask questions, and generate solutions • Focus on the content of the writing • Are patient, friendly, and focused on developing the student as a writer and thinker	• Are dominated by the teacher talking, without equal opportunities for students to engage • Position the teacher to identify and correct mistakes in the writing without including the student in problem-solving • Do not use dialogic strategies to encourage students to think more deeply about the content of the writing and how it is structured • Focus on the mechanics and grammar of the writing • Are rushed and may lack patience

Strategy #1: Preparing for and Facilitating Effective Writing Conferences

Writing conferences should be conversational. Remember, the goal is not for you the teacher to fix every error or solve composition problems, but to be a collaborator who helps students to identify areas of strength and areas for development.

Questions can be a non-threatening way for teachers to guide students in thinking critically about their writing to help them develop into expert learners who know their strengths, limitations, and areas of need as writers. The more teachers ask questions that encourage students to think deeply about their own writing and the writing process generally, the more likely it is these conferences will be effective. Students should come prepared with questions, and teachers should have a bank of questions they can draw from in conversations about student writing (see Table 7.2).

Table 7.2: Writing Conference Example Questions

Student Questions	Teacher Questions
Questions about the Writing Process	
• How can I make my writing more interesting and engaging for readers? • How can I improve my transitions between paragraphs, so the relationship between my ideas is clear? • What are some strategies I can use to revise my writing effectively? • How do I strengthen the arguments in my writing? • How can I make my writing more concise? Are there places where my writing feels too wordy? • How do I effectively integrate quotes and sources into my writing? • How do I develop my voice and tone in my writing? • How can I write more descriptive and vivid scenes or descriptions? • What common grammatical or syntax errors did I make that I should watch out for? • How can I organize my writing more effectively?	• Can you tell me more about your main idea or the message you are trying to communicate? • Who is the intended audience for your writing? • What do you want the reader to understand or take away from your writing? • What challenges are you facing while writing this piece? • Can you tell me more about your writing process? What strategies have helped you to complete this writing assignment? • Is there a specific section you are struggling with? Why do you think this part has been hard to write? • What aspects of your writing would you like to focus on improving? • What do you think is the strongest part of this composition? • Can you think of another way to approach this section?

Questions about the Content	
<ul><li>Can you explain this concept or idea in more detail?</li><li>How does this process work? Can you clarify the steps involved?</li><li>What are the causes of this phenomenon?</li><li>How has this issue evolved? How has public perception shifted?</li><li>What are some of the different perspectives or opinions on this issue?</li><li>Can you provide examples or direct me to resources to help me understand this better?</li><li>How has this concept or process changed over time?</li><li>What are the implications or consequences of this concept or process?</li><li>How does this relate to other similar concepts or processes?</li><li>What historical context or background might help me to better understand this event, person, or issue?</li></ul>	<ul><li>Can you explain the concept or process in simpler terms?</li><li>How does this connect to real-world examples or situations?</li><li>Can you compare and contrast this concept or process with another similar one?</li><li>What are the most important details or steps to remember when discussing this?</li><li>How has this concept or process changed or evolved?</li><li>Can you identify potential limitations or challenges with this concept, process, or argument?</li><li>What are the implications or applications of this concept or process?</li><li>What impact does this concept or process have on a particular field or industry?</li><li>How does this concept or process relate to your experiences or understanding of the world?</li></ul>

As students prepare for a writing conference, teachers should provide time in class for them to review their writing and generate or select three to five questions they want to ask during the writing conference. Younger students will need teachers' support as they articulate their questions, so this may work best in a small teacher-led group where the teacher can provide differentiated instruction and support. Older students may be able to complete this step with some initial guidance and a bank of questions to reference or draw from.

Students may want to work alone, with a partner, or as part of a small group. Teachers can build this pre-work into an offline station in a station rotation or include it in a writing playlist using a conference form like the one pictured in Table 7.3.

Students can ask questions focused on the writing process (e.g., structure, organization, mechanics) or the content their writing explores (e.g., concepts, processes, issues, phenomena). We encourage teachers to give students the agency to identify questions that will make this time together meaningful and help them progress toward clear writing objectives and develop strong conceptual knowledge.

Table 7.3: Writing Conference Form

Writing Conference Form		
Pre-conference	During the Conference	After the Conference
Write 3–5 questions you would like to discuss in this writing conference. (Need inspiration? Review the example questions.)	Make notes about what you are learning about the structure and content of your writing.	Reflect on the following questions using what you learned in the writing conference.
1. 2. 3. 4. 5.		1. The strongest part of my writing is . . . 2. The aspect of my writing that needs development is . . . 3. My plan for improving this piece of writing is . . .

During the conference, teachers can use a strategy called the "dialogic interview" to ensure each person has uninterrupted time to ask and answer questions. In a dialogic interview, the interviewer engages the interviewee in dialogue, using a specific set of questions or goals they want to achieve, while still allowing for a more open and exploratory conversation and relaxed flow. The emphasis is on creating a collaborative, back-and-forth exchange rather than a one-sided, question-and-answer dynamic. Teachers using this approach can invite students to begin by asking the questions they've written or selected as part of their pre-conference work, and the teacher can focus on responding, clarifying, explaining, etc.

Once the student has asked their questions, the teacher and student switch roles, with the teacher asking questions and the student responding. To keep the conversation flowing, the person answering questions should try to provide thorough responses. This technique may help teachers to avoid dominating the conference with too many questions and suggestions.

Teachers should encourage students to jot down any notes on their writing conference form that will help them revise their writing. Since the teacher and students may discuss many aspects of the writing process and the content of the writing, these notes will help students keep track of the important information, suggestions, and strategies they learned during the conference. Teachers can also invite students to record the conversation if that will be easier for them than writing or typing notes.

Following the conference, teachers should ask students to reflect on the experience and on what they learned about themselves as writers. Simply ask students to take a moment to fill in the following sentence stems.

1. The strongest part of my writing is . . .
2. The aspect of my writing that needs development is . . .
3. My plan for improving this piece of writing is . . .

This builds a reflective practice into the writing conference format, which is a critical step for students to develop into expert learners who know their strengths and limitations as writers.

Strategy #2: Embedding Writing Conferences in a Playlist

As students advance through a writing playlist, teachers can incorporate writing conferences that foster dialogue about students' writing. These conferences differ from the real-time feedback discussed in chapter 6, where the teacher provides feedback focused on a specific aspect of the student's writing. Instead, they offer a collaborative space where the teacher and student can exchange ideas and reflect on the writing process and content. Students receive formative feedback that enhances their writing skills while challenging their understanding of complex concepts, issues, texts, and phenomena in their subject areas. These conversations encourage students to reflect on their writing and delve deeper into their topics and questions so they can use writing across all subjects to make connections, explore topics, and apply critical thinking skills.

As discussed in chapter 6, the playlist model comprises a series of learning activities designed to move students toward a desired result or learning objective. A writing playlist may help students construct an argument, analyze a text, compare and contrast different concepts, describe the process and outcome of an experiment, or tell a captivating story.

A history teacher may want students to analyze and synthesize a collection of resources to construct informative writing. A math teacher might want students to demonstrate deep conceptual knowledge by writing a viable argument. An art teacher may have students analyze and evaluate how the artist's choices and techniques help to communicate a particular message or convey meaning. These are cognitively complex tasks, and students will need different amounts of time to complete a piece of formal writing. Some students can complete a writing assignment in a day or two, while others need a week or two. That makes the playlist model ideal because it gives students a high degree of control over their pacing as they compose a piece of writing.

When constructing a playlist, it is helpful to use the principles of backward design.[4] First, teachers should identify the desired results. What are students working toward? Second, they must decide on an assessment strategy that will help them measure progress toward that desired result or learning objective. How will they assess their students' understanding or skills? Finally, they need to construct a flexible learning path. What instruction, models, practices, supports, etc. will students need to transfer and apply their learning? How can the path provide meaningful choices to ensure all students progress toward firm standards-aligned writing goals?

AI-Enhanced Strategy: Technology-Based Thought Partner

Writing has a technical component that can be time-intensive to teach. Teachers outside of English language arts or world languages may not feel as confident correcting the mechanical aspects of writing. Even English teachers may want to focus, at times, more on the structure, organization, and content of a student's writing instead of getting distracted by the run-on sentences, missing punctuation, or homophone errors. So, it can be useful to teach students how to use tools like Grammarly to receive feedback on the mechanics of their writing.

We both appreciate having Grammarly running in the background of our Google Docs as we compose rough drafts of blog posts, articles, and these book chapters! Every writer makes mistakes (us included). Grammarly serves as a second pair of eyes on our writing. It catches everything from spelling errors to sentence structure issues to wordy statements that might be hard for the reader to understand. The beautiful thing about using it is that, unlike Word's spell-check function, it doesn't just identify the errors and suggest a change; it offers an explanation of what is not working in the writing and why. We have both gained a better understanding of ourselves as writers. One of us tends to split her infinitives (that's Cat), and one of us has a habit of inserting *that* unnecessarily (that's Katie—pun intended). As an example, in the following sentence, you don't need *that*.

Original: It's important to note that Katie has bad grammar habits.

Revision: It's important to note Katie has bad grammar habits.

Instead of fearing AI technology (since it is here to stay), teachers can use this technology as a resource to help students develop as writers. Teachers can show students how to use tools like ChatGPT and Grammarly to receive feedback on their writing. For example, I copied and pasted the first paragraph from this section into ChatGPT and asked, "How can I make this paragraph stronger?" ChatGPT suggested the following revision.

> Effective writing requires a mastery of both form and substance, and while the latter is typically emphasized in classrooms, the former is equally essential. However, teaching the technical aspects of writing can be challenging, especially for educators outside of English language arts or world languages. Even English teachers may struggle to balance the demands of correcting mechanical errors such as run-on sentences, missing punctuation, and homophone errors with the more substantive concerns of structure, organization, and content. To mitigate this, it is essential to equip students with the tools they need to self-correct. By teaching students how to use automated proofreading

and grammar-checking tools like Grammarly, educators can empower students to take ownership of their writing and become more proficient writers.

Not bad! The tone is more formal, but ChatGPT has elevated the vocabulary with words like *mitigate* and *substantive*. The paragraph also does a nice job of separating the idea of "form and substance" when it comes to the writing process. This revision provides some food for thought in terms of organization, transitions, and word choice. Writers who lack confidence may find this tool helps them understand how to communicate their ideas more effectively in writing.

Regardless of the technology tool students use to get feedback on their writing, that feedback should be used to encourage reflection and improvement.

Wrap-Up

The purpose of writing conferences is to provide personalized feedback and facilitate a collaborative dialogue between teacher and student about the student's writing. Writing conferences offer a range of benefits, including improved writing skills, increased confidence, enhanced motivation, opportunities for self-reflection, a better understanding of writing goals and objectives, and better relationships with teachers.

During these one-on-one sessions, the teacher provides guidance on specific areas of improvement, such as organization, content, and style. The teacher also helps students understand their writing goals and objectives, as well as the teacher's expectations. This can motivate students to continue developing their writing skills and foster a supportive relationship with the teacher. Writing conferences provide an opportunity for self-reflection, leading to further improvement and growth in the student's writing abilities. Before reflecting on and discussing the contents of this chapter, consider the strategies that were introduced:

- Strategy #1: Preparing for and Facilitating Effective Writing Conferences
- Strategy #2: Embedding Writing Conferences in a Playlist
- AI-Enhanced Strategy: Technology-Based Thought Partner

Reflect/Discuss

1. What are some benefits of having students generate questions to ask during a writing conference, and how can you support students in this process?
2. What is the dialogic interview strategy, and how can it be used during a writing conference to promote collaborative dialogue between you and your students?
3. How can you leverage writing conferences as a component of the playlist model to provide more opportunities for students to access formative feedback and promote reflective practice?
4. What are some ways in which students can reflect on their writing conference experience, and how can this reflective practice help them become expert learners?

Putting It into Practice

- Identify a writing assignment that will take students different amounts of time to complete. Then use backward design to create a writing playlist that will allow students to self-pace through this assignment while you facilitate writing conferences. Consider the following questions as you build your playlist:
    - What is the desired result or learning objective for this writing assignment?

- How will you measure student progress toward this learning objective or desired result?
- What will students need to progress toward this desired result or learning objective? What instruction, models, learning activities, support, etc. will you include in their learning path to support all students in making progress toward these learning objectives?
- At what point(s) in the writing process will it be valuable for students to meet with you for a writing conference to discuss their writing process and/or the content of their writing?

- Make a copy of the writing conference form provided in the online resources for this book, which you can access with the QR code at the front of the book, and modify it to use with your students.
  - What changes or adjustments will you need to make?
  - How will you onboard students to writing conferences?
  - What support, instruction, guidance, and/or models will they need to successfully engage in a writing conference?
- Then work on your own or with a colleague to generate a list of questions (and/or question stems) students might want to use to prepare for their writing conference.
- Finally, generate a list of questions you can use to encourage your students to think more deeply about the composition and content of their writing.
- Insert a link to the writing conference form and questions into your playlist to support students in preparing for and reflecting on their writing conferences.

8

The Power of Peer Feedback

The Blue Bin of Regret

Katie

As a secondary English teacher in the early 2000s, I made peace with the fact that I would be lugging home reams of paper each night in my LL Bean tote so I could pore over student papers. One of my mentor teachers actually had a milk crate with a handle that she wheeled around campus like she was headed to the airport. Every time she walked through the hallway, numerous colleagues yelled out, "Hope you don't miss your flight." Yep, that was what it was like if you wanted to assign student writing in the early-digital era. Not for the faint of heart.

While my friends were out slurping noodles at BYOB restaurants on Friday nights, I was cozied on the couch with a bag of Goldfish, an episode of *The Office*, and a stack of student papers taller than my cocker spaniel. After a week of putting on a show for teenagers through whole-class instruction, I was exhausted. I figured I should just get it done on Friday night so I could enjoy the rest of the weekend.

I had a set of purple pens (my signature color) that I used to painstakingly write the same comments over and over and over again. (I often debated investing in a custom set of stamps to save myself time.) As a teacher, you know the ones:

- Please read your paper aloud before handing it in to catch some of these errors.
- When citing evidence, remember to give credit to the author.
- Reread the prompt again before you revise. You did not address the prompt.
- Don't forget to write a conclusion that sums up your main arguments.

I recall the blurred vision, the hand cramps, and the madness of trying to figure out which student's report cover had lost its sliding lock. (Who invented those anyways?)

All the effort was worth it, I told myself. Students would reflect deeply on my feedback and become better writers . . . right? But you know how this story ends. On Monday morning, I would lovingly share my work with students only to see them literally stuff the papers into binders, make them into origami airplanes, or toss them in the blue recycling bin where my Friday night withered and died.

I had had it. I remember the day I decided I would no longer be the sole provider of feedback. I stomped into the next-door classroom, clutching the blue recycling bin to my chest, and slammed it on the octagon table.

"These students don't care how much time I spent providing feedback on their work!?" My teaching partner, Carol, a thirty-year veteran and the most fabulous teacher of all time, said something like, "Of course they don't. They are twelve. Maybe you should have them do the work themselves, so they appreciate how much thought goes into the feedback. It's a win-win. They learn more about revision, and you don't have to spend your weekends providing feedback no one reads." I pictured Carol snuggled up on her weekends with a glass of wine and a good book. She was on to something.

It seemed like an obvious solution, but the question nagged: "But how can I get them to give each other valuable feedback?" She responded, "You teach them how."

Research and Reality

One significant barrier that prevents content area teachers from incorporating more disciplinary writing in their courses is the workload created by commenting on and marking it all.[1] We have all likely dealt with the mental (and possibly physical) weight of taking home papers to provide feedback. Turns out, it's not only a time suck for us as teachers, but peer reviews are actually *more* beneficial.

In a study on peer feedback, researchers found that students—even young learners—who receive feedback from multiple peers improve their writing quality more than students receiving feedback from a single expert teacher.[2] Why, you ask? Because instructor feedback, particularly written feedback, is often ineffective, especially when instructors are overwhelmed by the demanding nature of writing assignments. Read: burnout and exhaustion are not great drivers of mastery-oriented feedback.

Now, to be clear, simply asking students to switch papers and make some comments will not transform writing. Peer review, like all skill sets, needs to be explicitly modeled, scaffolded, and reviewed. Before facilitating peer review, share the goals of the process. In addition to creating a culture where students share and reflect on each other's writing, peer review also supports students to become more critical readers. As they read peers' work with a critical eye, they can transfer the same process to their own writing to increase self-reflection and self-awareness.[3]

Without this support, there is a danger that students will make "low-hanging fruit" revisions—correcting misspellings and adding missing punctuation—rather than take on more difficult problems, such as reorganizing writing or inserting more convincing evidence. We can minimize the likelihood of low-hanging-fruit feedback by providing clear prompts, examples, and non-examples of high-quality feedback to support the peer-review process. In one study with multilingual learners, students were given peer-review prompts so they could provide feedback on drafts of peers' autobiographies. Prompts included:

- Is the thesis sentence in the first paragraph? If not, where is it? Write the thesis here.
- Are there any places the writer could be more clear? Be specific; make specific suggestions. What would you like to know more about?
- What do you think is the autobiographical significance of this writing? In other words, what can readers learn from it?[4]

After reflecting on the prompts, students received sample feedback with the instructions "Read each of the following peer comments about a partner's paper, and evaluate them for how helpful they would be in revising a paper." These examples and non-examples included:

- The summary isn't really a summary, but I like it anyway.
- Your story is OK.
- The first paragraph should be more detailed and catchy about what's going on in 1989.
- The details are sufficient.

Scaffolding the peer-review process with sample feedback that shows what helps writers reflect and revise will help students model those kinds of comments in their reflections. Note how in the example above, none of the prompts were yes/no questions.

Students who are new to peer review benefit from just-in-time feedback and support, which you can provide as an instructor by observing groups working on the peer-review process, or you can use a station rotation to pull small groups of students, to focus on their interactions and the quality of their feedback.

Kirsten Jamson, who leads the Center for Writing staff at the University of Wisconsin-Madison, shares the following advice for teachers as students engage in peer review.

> By observing how your students work in their groups and intervening to encourage careful listening and questioning, you can coach them to become better reviewers and writers. I recommend "hovering" around the groups to keep them on task. If the students are doing peer review for the first time, they will probably finish early and need to be prodded to spend more time on each paper. They may also be "too nice," avoiding tough questions and honest responses. Talking afterwards about what the groups did well—sharing good written reviews and using a skilled group as a model—can help students improve as peer reviewers.[5]

Strategy #1: Make the Rubric Work Double-Time

If you have a well-developed rubric, you can use it to drive peer review. For example, the following rubric in Table 8.1 can be used for argumentative writing. Teachers can add a peer review column to the rubric and transform it into a peer feedback tool. Not only does it provide students with a clear structure to look at each other's work, but using the rubric to guide peer review reinforces the students' understanding of the expectations of the writing assignment they are working on. This works especially well when students help generate the rubric as a component of pre-writing.

Table 8.1: Rubric to Drive Peer Review

Peer Review

Directions: Please use this rubric to assess your partner's argumentative writing. Circle the score you would give each element of this piece of writing and explain your reasoning.

- Why did you give this work the score you did on each criterion?
- What did you notice in the work that aligned with the level of mastery?
- How might this element be improved or developed?

Criteria	Beginning 1	Developing 2	Proficient 3	Mastery 4	Peer Review
Claim	Claim(s) is unclear. No clear reasons are given.	Claim(s) is clear, but the reasons are unclear, absent, or incomplete.	Claim(s) and reasons are clearly stated.	Claim(s) is clearly stated, and the reasons are strong.	
Evidence	Central claim is not supported. No evidence provided.	Attempts to support the central claim and reasons with facts, but information is unclear, inaccurate, or lacks citations.	Supports the central claim and reasons with facts, necessary details, and citations.	Supports the central claim and reasons with strong facts, thorough details, and accurate citations.	
Explanation	Contains little to no explanation or analysis of the information presented.	Attempts to explain and analyze the information, but the explanation is unclear or inaccurate.	Clearly explains and analyzes most of the information presented.	Clearly, concisely, and thoroughly explains and analyzes the information presented.	

Strategy #2: Balance Glows and Grows

It is important that we model effective feedback practices to our learners so they have strategies to balance well-deserved support, praise, and positivity with mastery-oriented feedback. We want every learner to feel connected with peers and validated for their growth while also having ideas for the next steps in their practice. In *The Shift to Student-Led*, we shared a choice board for peer review (Table 8.2), with a series of prompts focused on both glows and grows.

Table 8.2: Peer-Feedback Choice Board

Peer-Feedback Choice Board		
Directions: Select TWO prompts from the peer-feedback choice board to provide specific, meaningful, and kind feedback.		
Greatest Strength	**Tiny Tweaks**	**Celebrate Surprises**
Identify the strongest aspect of this draft. What specifically was strong? Why do you think this element was particularly powerful or well done? How did this element positively impact the overall quality of the writing?	Identify one aspect of this writing that would benefit from a minor revision, modification, or tweak. How would reworking this element impact the overall quality of the writing? Do you have specific recommendations for improving this aspect of their writing?	As you reviewed this draft, what surprised you about it? Was there an unexpected, original, outside-of-the-box, engaging, or particularly thought-provoking aspect of their work? Describe why you liked this aspect of their work.

Hungry for More	Mind Blown	Clarifying Confusion
Identify a part of the draft that needs further development. What would you have enjoyed knowing more about or having more information on? Where could more detail and development have strengthened this project? Can you identify the specific places in the writing where the student should spend time digging deeper?	Identify something in this draft that you loved and had not considered as you completed your draft. Is there a great idea or approach this student used that you would like to incorporate into your work? Why did you like this element of their writing? How can you incorporate this idea or approach into your revision?	As you reviewed this draft, was there anything unclear, confusing, or that left you wondering? Is there an aspect of this draft that you would like clarity on or more specifics about? Can you identify specific elements of this project that would benefit from clearer language and/or more explanation?

Choice Board Selection	Write your feedback below. Please be specific and kind.
Title of Feedback Prompt #1:	
Title of Feedback Prompt #2:	

It may also be helpful to share some sample responses so students can reflect on what type of feedback is validating and helpful to their own writing process. In Table 8.3, we share sample feedback provided to educators taking a graduate course on UDL. Although we both share feedback as a narrative, the table below separates the glows and grows to show how comprehensive and specific feedback can be. As you can see from the samples, glows allow peers to build relationships, share connections, and honor work that is universally designed. For mastery-oriented feedback, you may share a resource, ask a question, or suggest improvements. As a teacher, you can use feedback samples from your own practice, or you can create examples and non-examples so students can reflect on the type of feedback that would allow them to revise and improve their writing.

Table 8.3: Sample Glows and Grows from Peer Review

	Glows	Grows
Sample Feedback #1	Happy Monday. Your blog is right on—and your understanding and discussion of UDL is exactly on point. It is clear you understand the three core principles of UDL. You will be such an asset in your district as you help to build a calibrated understanding of UDL as a foundation for inclusive practice.	My brain always goes to how you can use this work in your school learning environment. So, for example, you could provide colleagues with the option to read or listen to your blog by just recording your own voice reading it on Vocaroo (https://vocaroo.com/). You could then provide a "buffet" of artifacts for them to learn more and then have them complete a protocol like the 4A protocol to discuss what they are learning and connecting it to your own practice. When you create work like this, find a way to put it into action so you can teach others and build a culture of shared understanding and learning! I'd love to know your thoughts on using something like this in a meeting or a PLC!

Sample Feedback #2	YES! I totally agree with everything in this reflection. It is such a disservice that so many people equate engagement to a simple "fun-meter" as opposed to a much more complex "worth committing to" meter. Teachers often talk about engagement as though we can somehow get every student to fall in love with all subject matter when it is much more important to help them to understand the purpose of the subject matter, to constantly put in the effort, and reflect and experience the value of growth and achieving something they didn't think was possible. It would also take so much stress off educators to try to make things "fun," as if we are camp counselors and not amazing educators!	I think it would be amazing if you took this one step further and created a list of concrete tips for teachers to increase student engagement in algebra. As much as teachers will agree with the blog, they may not know what to do next. So, it would be really great if you had a transition like "So how do we get students to stick with it? Here are some options/choices you can provide through the lens of UDL. While you implement these strategies, it is important to continue to monitor student engagement to determine if the actions you're taking are resulting in growth and more stickiness." Or something like that. Can't wait to see a revision!

Strategy #3: Hold a "Mock" Peer Review

To prepare students for the peer-review process, consider holding a "mock" peer review. To begin, provide all students with a writing exemplar. You could use a paper from a previous semester, produce a sample paper yourself (remember dogfooding?), or ask ChatGPT or another AI tool to create an exemplar for you. Then, ask students to spend five minutes reading the paper and ten minutes writing comments on a Padlet, shared slide deck, Post-its notes, etc. You can then use many different examples of visual artifacts to discuss whether the feedback is specific or non-specific and whether it would drive reflection and revision.

You can universally design this process by allowing students to access the exemplar digitally or in hard copy, work alone or with a partner or small group, or even split the class into two groups and facilitate a fish bowl so one half can listen while the other discusses their feedback. To facilitate a fishbowl discussion, divide your class into two groups, a small inner circle and an outer circle. The inner circle could have a discussion about the feedback they would provide on a particular piece of writing while the outer circle can listen and make notes. As the outer circle listens, they can focus on how well or poorly the first team worked together to share peer feedback. After a predetermined amount of time, the roles of the two circles are switched, so all students have opportunities to discuss peer feedback and actively listen to peers.

Strategy #4: Ask Students to Memorialize Peer-Review Sessions

Once students have an opportunity to reflect on the feedback from their peers, support them in memorializing their feedback by creating a plan for revision. After we wrote the first draft of this book, it was reviewed by our peers. We received a letter from our editor with all the comments generated during the peer-review process. After reading this letter, we connected to create a strategy for revision, determine action steps, and assign tasks so that we can collaborate throughout the revision process. If we just read the feedback and said, "Hey, thanks for the feedback," and then sent it to the blue recycling bin, we promise this book wouldn't be as strong. So, share with your students that the peer-review process is authentic and necessary, and it's important for them to translate feedback into action.

Students can memorialize their feedback in many ways. One possibility is to design a choice board (Table 8.4) with options.

Table 8.4: Memorialize Your Feedback

Memorialize Your Feedback		
After discussing the results of your draft with peers, reflect on any/all feedback you received from your peers. Summarize what you learned about your strengths and areas where you have the potential for incredible growth using one of the following choices. Once you complete it, add it to your digital portfolio!		
Recipe	**Dear Diary**	**Multimedia**
Create a recipe for success! Do you have a specific learning goal (or dish!) you want to work toward? What materials or strategies will you need to revise your writing? What ingredients will you need for this recipe? What steps will you need to follow to make this dish or accomplish this goal?	Write a diary entry sharing your strengths and areas where you will continue to focus your growth. What did you learn about your strengths from this feedback? What did the feedback teach you about the areas where you need to improve? What do you plan to do to act on this feedback? Your diary entry can be handwritten or digital.	Use audio or video to record a message to yourself about areas where you can continue to grow your practice as an expert writer. How can you take what you learned to continue to improve? What resources and strategies might you use in the future as you approach the writing process? What support might help you continue improving?

Alternatively, consider asking students to respond to the quality of the feedback they received. You could prompt them to answer questions like "What was the most valuable feedback?" and "What is one thing you learned about your own writing process from reflecting on the peer feedback?"

AI-Enhanced Strategy: Generate Questions to Guide Peer Editing

It can be challenging for teachers to generate questions for students to use when engaged in peer editing for a variety of reasons. First, writing prompts must be carefully crafted to ensure that they are both challenging and accessible to students of all skill levels. This requires a deep understanding of the students' abilities, interests, and learning preferences. Second, prompts must be specific enough to guide students in providing meaningful feedback on their peers' writing, while still allowing for creativity and personal expression. Finally, prompts must be varied and engaging to maintain students' interest and prevent them from becoming bored or disengaged with the peer-editing process. All of these factors make generating effective writing prompts a complex and difficult task for teachers, who are swamped with a million other tasks and responsibilities.

We asked ChatGPT to draft prompts to guide peer editing. The first time we asked for prompts for peer review for a second-grade class, ChatGPT only generated yes/no questions such as:

- Did the writer use capital letters at the beginning of each sentence?
- Did the writer end each sentence with punctuation?
- Did the writer use finger spaces between words?

This is more of a peer-editing checklist than a peer review, as the answers to these questions would not result in meaningful conversations about the text and revisions. Once we re-prompted that we wanted open-ended peer-review questions (again, for second grade), the following prompts were generated.

- What was your favorite part of your peer's writing? Why did you like it?
- Did your peer use any new words that you liked? Which words were they, and what do you think they mean?
- Which parts of your peer's writing did you find unclear? Can you ask them questions to help clarify?
- How was the writing similar to or different from the exemplar we reviewed?

Just like AI technology can serve as a thought partner for students, it can do the same for educators, saving them significant time generating powerful resources to support students.

Wrap-Up

Peer feedback is critical to the writing process, as it provides numerous opportunities for students to become more critical readers and to provide feedback to drive revisions. It also helps them become more aware of the components of high-quality writing. The bonus is that it also significantly minimizes educators' time spent providing feedback on student work. By shifting feedback practices to peers and scaffolding and providing feedback on those practices, we can create classrooms where students have opportunities for connection, revision, and reflection. The following strategies, discussed throughout this chapter, are great places to begin this shift.

- Strategy #1: Make the Rubric Work Double-Time
- Strategy #2: Balance Glows and Grows
- Strategy #3: Hold a "Mock" Peer Review
- Strategy #4: Ask Students to Memorialize Peer-Review Sessions
- AI-Enhanced Strategy: Generate Questions to Guide Peer Editing

Reflect/Discuss

1. Reflect on your current feedback practices. How much time do you spend providing feedback on student writing? What could you spend more time on if you shifted feedback practices to peer review?
2. How do you support your students to offer authentic and goal-oriented feedback to each other through the peer-review process?
3. What is one strategy in this chapter you will integrate into writing instruction in your learning environment?

Put It into Action

1. Identify an upcoming disciplinary writing prompt.
2. Draft at least four prompts to drive peer review (remember to avoid yes/no questions). You may want to use the examples provided in this chapter for inspiration.
3. Schedule a mock peer review where students use prompts to provide feedback on an exemplar. You may ask students to share their responses in a collaborative space (using Post-its and chart paper or a digital board like Padlet). If students share feedback in a collaborative space, provide opportunities for them to notice similarities and differences in the feedback provided.
4. Ask students to reflect on which feedback is most helpful and have them note what high-quality feedback has in common.
5. Once students have reflected on the mock feedback session, have them memorialize what they learned so they can apply it when they provide feedback to their peers, using the provided prompts, the assignment rubric, or a combination of both methods.

9

Self-assessment

She Had Me at Duck Boats

Catlin I'll never forget the early days of writing *UDL and Blended Learning* with Katie. I was shocked by how much we have in common. Our first dog was a fluffy white Samoyed. We both love to work out (she runs and I row) while listening to crime novels and murder mysteries on Audible. Even though we were both English teachers, we often share audiobook recommendations that are not going to win any National Book Awards. We just want to be entertained with mindless fun while we sweat! We are passionate about strong coffee, high heels, and international travel.

As much as Katie and I have in common, we were very different writers. I wake up early, hours before my kids get up for school, and knock out my writing before the sun comes up. By contrast, Katie seems to do her best work at night, after her kids go to bed. I would wake up each morning to a message, like "This chapter is ready for you, Cat!"

I remember the morning she sent me a revised version of our introduction. She added a story about the duck boats in Boston,

Massachusetts, that are popular with tourists who want to explore the historical landmarks dotting the city. She highlighted the duck boats' versatility as they drive through Boston's busy streets and float right into the bay. Katie's story transported me back in time to a trip I took to Boston with my good friend, JP. I remember being bundled up in our winter coats, cold air stinging our faces and plastic duck whistles in our mouths. We had a ball riding around the city in a duck boat, blowing into our ridiculous yellow duck whistles, whistling at people we passed—"QUAAAAACK!"—and giggling uncontrollably! Then, as easily as she had painted this picture of Boston for me, she said teachers needed mindsets, skill sets, and toolsets that were as flexible as the duck boats so they could teach with confidence in person, online, or a blend of the two. I was floored. How did she do that? She drew me in with a relatable story and used that story to pinpoint why we were writing this book for educators. I was in awe.

I went back to my draft of chapter 1 and reread the story I had been working on. Ugh. It was *not* good. It lacked details and description. The tone was too formal and did not communicate my personality at all. And it was a story about my experience as a teacher, not a story about my life. I deleted it and started over.

Before taking another stab at it, I reread Katie's story and made a list of all the things I found compelling, like the specific names of places in Boston and the details—"golden-domed" and "cobblestoned streets." I noted all the places where her personality shone through her writing. Then, I thought about the purpose of my story. I wanted to make the point that a lot of technology in and of itself does not equate to blended learning or a student-centered learning environment.

So, I spent hours brainstorming story ideas from my life that would be relevant and entertaining. I finally landed on a failed date night with my husband. I wrote about booking a cooking class at culinary school, describing the fully stocked professional kitchen we worked in and the well-known chef who guided the experience. And even though we had everything a person could want or need to cook, I did not enjoy the experience. As I wrote and rewrote the story, I focused on adding descriptive details, inserting dialogue, and describing my uncensored, honest reaction to the whole experience. It took multiple rounds of editing for me to get to a place where I was proud of the piece and felt confident it made my point.

Katie is a natural storyteller. I am not. I have written many books, but they have not included stories about my life. It is something I have to work at. When I read her stories or listen to her analogies when she works with educators, I marvel at her natural gift for storytelling. By contrast, I will always have to look at my narrative writing with a critical eye, analyzing what I have done well, what is missing, and what needs development to tell a compelling story. Yet, the more time I spend with each piece assessing my own writing, the more I learn about myself as a writer and the more confident I am as I write the next story.

Not all students will be natural writers. The process may present myriad challenges or stretch them in uncomfortable ways. Self-assessment is one vehicle we can use to help them understand their strengths, limitations, and areas where they would benefit from additional support. We may not all be natural storytellers or writers, but it doesn't mean we cannot cultivate those skills with support, practice, and reflection.

Research and Reality

In traditional teacher-led classrooms, students are the receivers. They receive information and instruction. They receive rubrics, feedback, and grades. They may not have opportunities to actively engage in these processes, which we think is a missed opportunity. As we laid out in our last book, *The Shift to Student-Led*, we want students to take an active role in their learning, and that includes assessment.

Too often the job of thinking about student learning and progress falls squarely on the teacher. And any teacher whose students write regularly knows that it creates a daunting amount of work to review, provide feedback on, and assess. When teachers do the lion's share of this work, it robs students of the opportunity to learn more about themselves and develop into expert writers. Without regular opportunities to think critically about their writing and engage in self-assessment practices, they are unlikely to develop a deep understanding of themselves as learners or writers.

Amy Siegesmund, a professor of biology at Pacific Lutheran University, defines self-assessment and identifies its benefits this way:

> Self-assessment is a reflective process where students use criteria to evaluate their performance and determine how to improve . . . Self-assessment is meant to be formative and help students improve subsequent performance. It has been demonstrated that self-assessment is critical for both current and lifelong learning . . . [It] increases self-motivation . . . empowers students to take responsibility for their learning . . . and leads to increases in student learning . . . Because the process of self-assessment increases metacognition . . . students also become more proficient at evaluating their progress toward completing a task, a key facet of self-regulated learning.[1]

Despite the clear benefits that self-assessment has on students' performance, metacognition, self-regulation, and motivation, there are many reasons why teachers may not dedicate time to it in the classroom.

First, teachers feel intense pressure to prepare students for standardized exams, cover adopted curricula with fidelity, or keep up with rigid pacing guides that do not leave time for metacognitive skill-building activities, like self-assessment. However, that concern does not take into consideration the positive impact self-assessment has on academic performance generally, or writing specifically. Self-assessment is "a means by which teachers help students become more metacognitive about their writing and writing processes, but they also often attempt to mitigate the negative effects of grading or testing writing."[2] Research also indicates that a regular practice of self-assessing writing leads to significant improvement in the content, language, and organization of students' writing.[3] In addition to improvements in the writing itself, self-assessment is linked to improved self-regulation skills and increased use of metacognitive strategies, like planning, monitoring, and evaluating writing.[4] It can have a positive impact on the student's motivation to write, as they have a better understanding of the process and how to improve their skills.[5] So, if teachers are working to prepare students for standardized exams or guide them through curriculum, both of those will be enhanced by a regular self-assessment practice. An increasing number of standardized exams require that students write to demonstrate their learning, and many state-adopted curricula integrate writing because, as we established in chapter 2, writing is linked to learning. So, dedicating class time to self-assessment can positively impact student performance on both fronts.

Teachers may also worry that students do not have the skills necessary to complete a meaningful self-assessment practice or are too young for metacognitive skill building. Yet, research shows that even elementary students benefit from self-assessment practice. In fact, researchers argue that this formative assessment is often overlooked with younger students, even though it gives them a voice and ownership over their learning, helps them develop into critical and reflective thinkers, and increases their motivation and achievement.[6] The benefits of self-appraisal or self-evaluation on engagement and academic performance in elementary school make a strong case for starting this metacognitive work early. That requires teachers to teach these skills the same way they approach teaching any other skill. Students need instruction on how to complete a self-assessment. They will need to see a model and listen to their teacher conduct a think-aloud while demonstrating this process. In the early stages of engaging in self-assessment, they will benefit from support and scaffolds, guided practice, and feedback in a teacher-led station.

Like any other skill, teaching students, especially younger students, how to think critically about and evaluate their work takes time and practice. The payoff is a fundamental shift in the perception of who should be thinking about student work, progress, and learning. Self-assessment shifts students from being dependent on and expecting teachers to always provide external prompts, feedback, and guidance, helping them to develop into independent, self-directed learners capable of evaluating their own work against clear success criteria or standards and of using what they learn about themselves to improve their performance.

Strategy #1: Self-assessment with the Rubric

Not only do rubrics focus the grading process on clear, standards-aligned criteria, they also work well as self-assessment tools, even for elementary students. A study that encouraged elementary students to look at examples of writing to generate success criteria (as we discussed in chapter 4), then use rubrics to conduct self-assessments led to significant improvements in their writing.[7] It makes sense that when students understand how to be successful on a writing assignment and have a clear rubric to guide them from the early stages through self-assessment, they will create more effective writing.

An effective rubric is composed of three parts: 1) a list of criteria aligned with standards or success criteria, 2) different levels of performance or mastery, 3) a clear, student-friendly description of what each criterion looks like at each level of performance or mastery. Research indicates that using these types of rubrics to facilitate a self-assessment practice can have a positive impact on a student's feelings of self-efficacy and their ability to self-regulate.[8] Teachers can use rubrics to engage students in the process of thinking critically about their work and evaluating its quality prior to a final summative assessment.

To make it easy for students to self-assess using a writing rubric, teachers can simply make a copy of their rubric and insert an additional "self-assessment score" column, like the math rubric for constructing viable arguments pictured in Figure 9.1. This rubric is based on California's math standards for practice:

> Mathematically proficient students understand and use stated assumptions, definitions, and previously established results in constructing arguments. They make conjectures and build a logical progression of statements to explore the truth of their conjectures. They are able to analyze situations by breaking them into cases, and can recognize and use counterexamples. They justify their conclusions, communicate them to others, and respond to the arguments of others. They reason inductively about data, making plausible arguments that take into account the context from which the data arose.[9]

To avoid overwhelming students, the rubric has three criteria: 1) begins with a conjecture/claim, 2) presents a logical progression of statements, and 3) justifies conclusions with clear reasoning and data. Then each of those criteria are described at each level of mastery. For example, in the beginning stages of writing, students may have an absent conjecture/claim, or it may not address the question. By the time students progress to mastery, their conjecture/claim is clear and thoroughly addresses the question.

The goal of these mastery-level descriptions is to help students understand what they are working toward, so teachers may need to do some focused work around the academic or subject-specific vocabulary that appears in their rubrics. Students may not know what *conjecture* means, for example, which would make it hard for them to present a clear one at the start of their written response. Instruction (video or small-group) on what this word means and how to present a conjecture or claim in writing is critical in the early stages of any written assignment. Even words like *analysis*, which teachers frequently use to talk about the writing process, may be opaque to students, who will need clarification to understand what they are being asked to do in their writing.

Teachers can print the self-assessment version of their writing rubric out or allow students to capture their self-assessments online. As they review their writing, they need to think about what they wrote in relation to the success criteria on the rubric and circle the language that they think best aligns with their writing. Once they have circled a specific level of performance or mastery for each criterion, they need to write a short explanation for the score they gave themselves. Why did they give themselves this score? What did they see in their work that made them think this was an appropriate score? Where do they want to focus their energy as they revise their writing? This written explanation motivates students to think critically about their work, read the descriptions of each level of performance or mastery closely, and justify their choice using details from their writing to support their self-assessment scores. Teachers may also want to add some reflective prompts or sentence stems for students to complete, like the ones pictured below the rubric in Figure 9.1. This pairs self-assessment with a reflective practice, so students spend a few minutes thinking about what they learned about themselves and their skill set from completing this reflection.

Using the same writing rubric to facilitate formative self-assessment that the teacher plans to use for the summative assessment has several clear benefits. First, it helps students to develop an increased awareness and understanding of the success criteria and evaluation scale. The more time students spend thinking about their writing through the lens of the criteria on a rubric, the more likely they are to identify specific areas of weakness and areas of strength. When this self-assessment happens in advance of a summative assessment, it also gives students the time and space to develop and revise their work before it is formally assessed. They can even seek out peer or teacher support as they work on their revision, which encourages self-advocacy for their specific needs.

Self-assessment scores can be useful reference points when having conversations with students about their progress. If a student has given themselves a significantly higher or lower score than you would have on a specific skill, this may signal that the student does not understand what is expected, is being too critical of their work, or needs additional support. This creates transparency around student progress and presents an opportunity for a conversation about what the students need to continue making progress toward mastery of specific skills.

Figure 9.1: Math Self-assessment Rubric: Constructing Viable Arguments

Math Self-assessment Rubric: Constructing Viable Arguments

Directions: Use this rubric to assess your mathematical writing. Circle the language that best describes where you are in relation to each criterion, then write a sentence explaining your choice in the self-assessment column. When you are done, please complete the reflection below.

Criteria	Beginning 1	Developing 2	Proficient 3	Mastery 4	Self-Assessment
Begins with a Conjecture/Claim	The conjecture or claim is absent or does not address the question.	The conjecture or claim is unclear or incomplete.	The conjecture or claim addresses the question.	The conjecture or claim is clear and thoroughly addresses the question.	
Presents a Logical Progression of Statements	The progression of statements does not present a logical sequence of ideas to support your conjecture/claim.	The progression of statements is hard to follow, lacks transitions, and does not effectively support your conjecture/claim.	The progression of statements presents a logical sequence of ideas that effectively support your conjecture/claim.	The progression of statements presents a clear and compelling sequence of ideas that effectively support your conjecture/claim.	
Justifies Conclusions with Clear Reasoning and Data	Lacks the necessary data, analysis, and reasoning to support the conclusions presented in this piece of writing.	Includes some data but limited analysis and reasoning needed to support the conclusions presented in this piece of writing.	Includes the necessary data, analysis, and reasoning to support the conclusions presented in this piece of writing.	Includes strong data, analysis, and reasoning to justify the conclusions presented in this piece of writing.	

Reflection:
One thing I did well in this paragraph was
One thing I struggled with while writing this paragraph was
One thing I could use more help with is

Strategy #2: Self-assessment Journal or Blog

Journaling is a powerful vehicle for driving reflection and fostering a deeper understanding of one's self. When teachers use journals or blogs to encourage regular reflective practice, that writing becomes documentation of the student's ongoing growth over time. The goal of a writing journal specifically is to help students develop their metacognitive muscles in relation to their writing. We want them to look closely at their writing to understand themselves better: their strengths, limitations, and growth.

Journaling at key moments in the writing process can help students approach writing with a higher level of intentionality. It can be used in the early stages of planning writing to brainstorm ideas, access prior knowledge, or generate a list of reasons to support a claim. In the middle of the writing process, asking students to pause and think about what they feel is working in their writing and what they are struggling with can also illuminate those areas where they feel confident and those where they feel they need more support. Students who feel particularly strong composing a piece of writing may be able to act as peer coaches. If students are struggling with an aspect of writing, it's helpful for the teacher if students can communicate their needs. That way, teachers can pull students who need support with a particular aspect of writing into their teacher-led station for small-group instruction and feedback.

When teachers ask students to journal about their writing, it can be helpful to group journal prompts into three categories: 1) content, 2) process, and 3) self-regulation. As students write, be it an argumentative paragraph, lab report, DBQ, or compare/contrast, they have to draw on and use their content knowledge to support their ideas, so reflective questions about content encourage them to assess their understanding of key concepts, processes, issues, and phenomena. This can help students appreciate the role that understanding the subject-area content has in constructing strong pieces of writing.

Process questions ask students to reflect on and describe how they approached a particular writing task, what strategies they used, and what worked well versus what didn't work. These questions can help students develop a deeper awareness of the strategies and resources available to them as they write. It can also help them to identify the specific aspects of the writing process they are struggling with, so they can advocate for their needs.

Self-regulation questions are focused on helping students evaluate their writing goals, feelings about writing, and their behavior and decisions as they worked on the writing assignment. These questions help students to understand themselves as people and writers in order to make choices that are likely to help them be successful (see Table 9.1).

Teachers can make time for these reflections by dedicating an online or offline station in a station rotation lesson to a reflective activity or inserting reflection prompts into a writing playlist to encourage students to pause and think about their writing at key moments during the process. We encourage teachers to make time for reflection in class instead of sending reflection prompts home with students. Teachers send a clear message about what they value by what they dedicate class time to, so it's important that students see this reflection as a vital part of their learning experience.

Table 9.1: Journal Prompts for Self-assessment

Journal Prompts		
Content	**Process**	**Self-regulation**
• What ideas or concepts did you need to understand to write this? • Were any of the ideas and concepts challenging to understand or write about? • What resources (e.g., book, article, video, podcast, experiment) did you draw your information or evidence from? Why did you select these particular sources to pull from? • How did completing this writing assignment improve your understanding of the concepts or ideas in this unit?	• What strategies did you use to prepare for this writing assignment? • How did you organize your ideas before beginning the writing process? • What resources did you use to compose this piece? • After completing a draft, how did you approach editing and revising this piece? • What aspect of writing this draft was the most challenging? What strategies did you use to navigate these challenges?	• What goal did you have for yourself as you began this piece of writing? • What decisions did you make that helped you complete this writing task? • How did you feel while writing this piece? What contributed to these feelings? • How well did you manage your time while writing? • If you got stuck, what did you do that helped?

Strategy #3: 3-2-1 Self-assessment

A simple 3-2-1 self-assessment can help students think more deeply about the feedback they received and what they learned about themselves as writers from it. Teachers can ask students to capture a 3-2-1 self-assessment, like the one pictured in Table 9.2, in their notebooks, a journal or blog, or an audio recording.

Table 9.2: 3-2-1 Writing Self-assessment

3-2-1 Writing Self-assessment	
3 Things I Did Well	
2 Things I Need to Revise or Improve	
1 Thing I Need Help With	

The more intentional we are in having students think critically about their writing and capturing what they learn about themselves using a self-assessment or reflective practice, the more likely students are to appreciate their growth. If they feel they are improving as writers, that will motivate them to stick with more challenging writing tasks and to appreciate how the work they are doing is contributing to the development of their writing skills.

AI-Enhanced Strategy: Designing Standards-Aligned Rubrics to Guide Self-assessment

Rubrics create a roadmap for success that students can use to guide their work on writing assignments. The best rubrics limit the number of criteria to avoid overwhelming learners. They also clearly describe

Self-assessment

what learning looks like at different levels of mastery: beginning, developing, proficient, and mastery.

Like most teacher tasks, designing a rubric can take significant time. This is where AI technology, like ChatGPT, can be incredibly helpful. Teachers can take the language from their standards to create standards-aligned, mastery-based rubrics in a fraction of the time it would have taken before AI.

Here is how it works. First, copy and paste your state standards for a writing assignment into ChatGPT. Here's what it looked like when Catlin did that.

> Catlin: Can you create a 4-point mastery-based rubric for these standards on argumentative writing, keeping the format at each level uniform? Please make each point its own criteria and combining similar ideas.
>
> - Write arguments to support claims in an analysis of substantive topics or texts, using valid reasoning and relevant and sufficient evidence.
> - Develop claim(s) and counterclaims fairly, supplying evidence for each while pointing out the strengths and limitations of both in a manner that anticipates the audience's knowledge level and concerns.
> - Write arguments to support claims in an analysis of substantive topics or texts, using valid reasoning and relevant and sufficient evidence.
> - Use words, phrases, and clauses to link the major sections of the text, create cohesion, and clarify the relationships between claim(s) and reasons, between reasons and evidence, and between claim(s) and counterclaims.
> - Write arguments to support claims in an analysis of substantive topics or texts, using valid reasoning and relevant and sufficient evidence.

- Establish and maintain a formal style and objective tone while attending to the norms and conventions of the discipline in which they are writing.
- Write arguments to support claims in an analysis of substantive topics or texts, using valid reasoning and relevant and sufficient evidence. Provide a concluding statement or section that follows from and supports the argument presented.

ChatGPT responded by identifying four main criteria for this writing assignment, based on the language of the standards. It wasn't exactly what Catlin asked it to do, but it helped sort through the clutter of all these aspects of argumentative writing to identify four criteria she might want to assess. This is where the teacher, as a subject-area expert, needs to decide whether the criteria identified are the ones they want to assess.

Catlin asked ChatGPT to break down each criterion it had identified into four levels of mastery and explicitly told it she wanted a beginning, developing, proficient, and mastery level. It generated this for the first criteria, "Claim and Evidence."

> Catlin: Now can you break each of these four criteria into four levels of mastery: beginning, developing, proficient, mastery?
>
> ChatGPT: Sure, here is a breakdown of each of the four criteria into four levels of mastery:
>
> 1. Claim and Evidence
>   - Beginning: Presents a claim that is not fully focused or substantiated by evidence, and does not adequately acknowledge counterclaims or anticipate audience concerns.

- Developing: Develops a claim that is somewhat focused and supported by some evidence, but does not fully acknowledge counterclaims or anticipate audience concerns.
- Proficient: Develops a clear and focused claim that is substantiated by relevant and sufficient evidence, presents counterclaims and acknowledges their strengths and limitations, and anticipates the audience's knowledge level and concerns.
- Mastery: Develops an exceptional claim that is exceptionally focused and supported by outstanding and extensive evidence, presents counterclaims and evaluates their strengths and limitations in great detail, and anticipates the audience's knowledge level and concerns with outstanding nuance and insight.

2. Coherence and Cohesion
    - Beginning: The argument is poorly organized, and connections between claims, reasons, and evidence are unclear. Transitions are absent or ineffective.
    - Developing: The argument is somewhat organized, and connections between claims, reasons, and evidence are somewhat clear. Transitions are present but are not always effective.
    - Proficient: The argument is well-organized and coherent, with clear connections between claims, reasons, and evidence. Transitions are effective and help guide the reader through the argument.
    - Mastery: The argument is exceptionally well-organized and coherent, with outstanding connections between claims, reasons, and evidence. Transitions are exceptional and make the argument flow seamlessly.

3. Style and Tone
    - Beginning: The style is informal and inappropriate for the discipline, and the tone is biased or subjective.
    - Developing: The style is somewhat appropriate for the discipline, but could be improved, and the tone is somewhat objective, but some bias or subjectivity remains.
    - Proficient: The style is appropriate for the discipline, and the tone is objective and unbiased throughout the argument. The language is clear and concise.
    - Mastery: The style is exceptionally appropriate for the discipline, and the tone is exceptionally objective and unbiased. The language is exceptionally precise and conveys ideas exceptionally clearly.

4. Concluding Statement
    - Beginning: The concluding statement is absent or poorly developed, and does not follow logically from the argument presented.
    - Developing: The concluding statement is somewhat developed, but could be more convincing or better supported by evidence.
    - Proficient: The concluding statement is well-developed and convincing, and follows logically from the argument presented. It summarizes the main points of the argument and uses evidence to support the conclusion.
    - Mastery: The concluding statement is exceptionally well-developed and exceptionally convincing, and follows logically and seamlessly from the argument presented. It summarizes the main points of the argument with exceptional clarity and nuance, and uses outstanding evidence to support the conclusion.

Again, the answer here isn't an example of something a teacher can copy, paste, and reuse without edits. There are words like *substantiated* that students may not understand. Since the goal of the rubric is to create a student-friendly roadmap for success, teachers will need to read through the language closely, revising it to work for their audience. In fact, you can ask ChatGPT to reword a section in "more student-friendly language" to ensure your learners can understand what is expected of them.

> Catlin: Can you rewrite this in more student-friendly language?
>
> ChatGPT: Sure, here is a more student-friendly version:
>
> Claim and Evidence
>
> - Beginning: You make a statement or claim, but it's not really clear or supported by evidence. You also don't talk about other possible viewpoints or what your audience might think.
>
> - Developing: You make a statement or claim that's kind of clear and has some evidence, but you don't really talk about other possible viewpoints or what your audience might think.
>
> - Proficient: You make a clear and focused statement or claim that has good evidence to back it up. You also talk about other possible viewpoints and explain their strengths and weaknesses. You consider what your audience might know or think about the topic.
>
> - Mastery: You make an exceptional and focused statement or claim that's supported by outstanding and extensive evidence. You also talk about other possible viewpoints in detail and evaluate their strengths and

> weaknesses. You show a deep understanding of what your audience might know or think about the topic.

Let's face it—writing is hard, and creating assignments, exemplars, and rubrics can be just as challenging. AI technology can be a game-changer for teachers and students alike. Teachers who leverage AI technology can provide their students with more personalized support and make the writing process less daunting for everyone involved. Rather than fearing the rise of AI, we'd love to see educators embrace it and see it as an opportunity to enhance the learning experience and reimagine when, where, and how writing takes place. As technology continues to develop and improve, we can make teaching more sustainable and learning more engaging than ever before.

Wrap-Up

Teachers play a vital role in guiding and assessing student writing, but it is equally important to empower students to take ownership of their own learning and development as writers. Self-assessment is a crucial component of metacognitive skill-building and should be integrated into classroom instruction. By dedicating class time to self-assessment, students can better understand their strengths and weaknesses as writers and develop a deeper understanding of the writing process.

Emphasizing the role of self-assessment in the writing process also reinforces the reality that learning is a shared responsibility between teacher and student. Educators can provide guidance and feedback, but students must also take an active role in their own development. By fostering a culture of self-assessment in the classroom, using the strategies listed below, teachers can empower students to take control of their own writing and become more confident, competent writers.

- Strategy #1: Self-assessment with the Rubric

- Strategy #2: Self-assessment Journal or Blog
- Strategy #3: 3-2-1 Self-assessment
- AI-Enhanced Strategy: Designing Standards-Aligned Rubrics to Guide Self-assessment

Reflect/Discuss

1. How often do you ask students to engage in self-assessment?
2. Which of the strategies presented in this chapter is most appealing to you? Why do you think this strategy would work well with your students? How can you give students agency in relation to this strategy? Can you build in a meaningful choice about how they approach self-assessment or capture their reflections?
3. What instruction or modeling might students need to begin using this strategy? What supports or scaffolds might students need to be successful with this self-assessment strategy?
4. What impact might a regular practice of self-assessment have on your students' attitudes about writing? How might the reflections they share help you design differentiated or personalized learning experiences?

Put It into Practice

Select a self-assessment strategy presented in this chapter and decide which blended learning model you will use to encourage your students to complete this task in class. You can build it into a station rotation, whole-group rotation, or playlist model. Finally, create the supports and scaffolds that students might need to successfully complete this self-assessment. Will they need to see a model or benefit from guided practice? Will sentence stems or feedback help them feel supported in the early stages of self-assessment?

Once you have your self-assessment strategy and know which blended learning model you'll use to engage student in this practice, share it with a colleague or your personal learning network for feedback.

10

Side-by-Side Writing Assessments

Snapchat-Worthy Meals

Catlin Before having children, I loved to cook! A few nights each week, I chose a fun recipe, played music or listened to NPR, and poured a glass of wine. It was a relaxing way to end the day.

Then I became a mom, and I had to cook dinner every single night. Cooking for my kids is a pretty thankless job. I imagine it's akin to preparing a meal for two cranky food critics. Almost every day on the car ride home from school or soccer practice, I get the question "What are we having for dinner tonight?" I wish I could accurately convey the apprehension and concern in their voices as they ask me this. If the answer isn't pasta, pizza, tacos, or burgers, I find myself on the receiving end of eye rolls, loud, annoyed sighs, or robust arguments for why we should eat something else. They quite literally suck the joy out of cooking!

Last year as I navigated a post-divorce reality and found myself juggling all of the responsibilities I used to share with my ex-husband, I was exhausted and realized I needed to find a different way to approach cooking that was more rewarding and less stressful. Enter the meal kit!

I decided that once a week my teenagers would prepare dinner with me. However, I did not want them to always make pasta or cook a frozen pizza. I wanted them to learn how to prepare healthy meals. So, I signed up for a meal kit service. (There are many, but I went with Green Chef.) My kids select a meal each week from the menu, choosing something that sounds good to them. Then I work with my teen to prepare the meal they selected.

The goal of shifting cooking from my sole responsibility to a shared responsibility was threefold. First, I wanted my kids to learn how to cook, since that's an important life skill, and without me and a microwave, they would likely starve. Second, I wanted them to develop an appreciation for the time and energy cooking requires because I had been busting my butt for years in the kitchen with zero recognition. Third, I hoped it would allow me to connect with my children individually.

The experiment was a success! I remember the first night I cooked with my son, thirteen, who chose a salmon and sautéed vegetable dish. (I was shocked!) He closely followed the directions, meticulously chopped vegetables, and asked questions about which oil to use and why. It was so enjoyable watching him navigate his first recipe. And he talked. Instead of the normal grunts I get when asking about his day, sports, friends, etc., he was chatty and engaging.

Not only was the experience of cooking with my child thoroughly enjoyable, but he was clearly proud of himself and the meal he made, as evidenced by the photo he took of his dinner that he shared with his friends on Snapchat. It was one of those parenting moments where I realized that I didn't need to do it all on my own. Cooking with my children is a much more rewarding and enjoyable experience than cooking by myself.

Like parenting, there are some teaching responsibilities that educators have classically done in isolation. Grading is probably the most time-consuming and thankless teacher task we take into our lives beyond the classroom. Yet, like cooking with my kids, grading can be an opportunity for connection and relationship building if teachers shift grading into the classroom.

I remember reading a quote by Margaret Heritage where she talked about the origins of the word *assessment*. It comes from the Latin word meaning "to sit with," and she makes the point that assessment is something we should do with and for students. Not only does grading with students create clarity about what they are doing well and where they need to invest more time and energy, but it also lightens the teacher's workload. It's a win-win, just like my approach to cooking with my kids!

Research and Reality

"If I don't grade it, students won't do it." We regularly hear this statement from educators when discussing the problems with traditional grading practices. The idea that students won't do work unless there are points attached is problematic on several levels. First, it suggests that the only motivation to complete assignments is the points students will receive. That is only the case if students do not understand the value of the work they are being asked to do or if it is not interesting or relevant to their lives.

In his book *Drive*, Daniel Pink, an author and speaker known for his work on motivation, creativity, and the changing world of work, talks about the limitations of using "carrots" or, in the context of school, grades, as a vehicle to motivate students to do work. Grades are an extrinsic motivator that may work for some students or for a short time, but they will never be as powerful as internal motivators. They may even create an incentive to submit work that isn't theirs. As Pink says, "The problem with making an extrinsic reward the only destination that matters is that some people will choose the quickest route there, even if it means taking the low road . . . When the reward is the activity itself—deepening learning . . . there are no shortcuts."[1]

Just as the internal motivators of enjoyment of a person's work, a sense of genuine achievement, and personal growth result in higher levels of job satisfaction, the same can be said for students and learning. Instead of relying solely on external motivators like grades or fear of punishment to entice students to do work, we should ask questions:

- How do we ensure the work we ask students to do feels meaningful and relevant to their lives?
- How can we build systems into our classroom that help them to foster autonomy and encourage students to drive their learning?
- How can we encourage students to recognize, appreciate, and share their progress and achievements?
- How can we integrate metacognitive skill building into our classrooms to help students track their progress and understand their growth?

Another issue with traditional grading practices is that teachers often assess aspects of student work that fall into the compliance category and using overly general criteria, like "effort," that do not focus on grade-level, subject-area standards. Grading that is not clearly linked to specific criteria or standards also contributes to the implicit bias—race, gender, class—that is well documented in research on grading practices.[2] For example, in a recent study, teachers were randomly assigned to receive one of two versions of a writing sample that talked about the author's brother. The samples were identical, except for the brother's name. In one version, the student author refers to his brother as "Dashawn," signaling a Black author; in the other, his brother is called "Connor," signaling a white author. Teachers were asked to holistically assess the paper, which led to biased results. Teachers shown the "Dashawn" version of the writing sample were 4.7 percentage points less likely to rate it as being on grade-level or above, compared to teachers shown the "Connor" version. However, when those same teachers used a rubric with specific grading criteria, they gave essentially identical ratings to the Black and white authors.

The results of this study argue that the best way to combat the inherent bias and subjectivity involved in the grading process is to focus on specific, standards-based criteria. Grades should reflect academic achievement and serve as a vehicle for students to better understand themselves and their progress toward firm, standards-aligned goals.

In his book *How to Grade for Learning*, Ken O'Connor, a Canadian education consultant and author who is best known for his work in the area of assessment and grading, emphasizes the value of including students in the grading process to create transparency around progress and to maximize the impact of grades.[3] Unfortunately, most teachers do not grade while collaborating with students. They grade in isolation during their preparation periods or at home on their evenings and weekends. It creates a ton of take-home work for teachers that robs them of the time they need to rest, relax, and recharge, while placing students in the powerless position of receiving grades they may not understand or know how to improve.

Teachers who attempt to grade everything students work on may be so exhausted by the first round of grading that they do not have the time or energy to allow students to edit, revise, and resubmit work. Yet, if educators want students to embrace a growth mindset in which they understand that they can continually improve with effort and practice over time, then we should be prioritizing revisions and encouraging resubmissions.[4] Teachers must be strategic about what they grade and where they grade. Instead of investing significant time grading work that falls into the category of review and practice, teachers should consider strategies for positioning students to look critically at and self-assess that work. Then teachers would be freed to invest their finite time and energy in assessing specific, standards-aligned criteria for work that is an actual assessment designed to measure progress toward those clear learning goals.

Side-by-side assessments pull grading into the classroom to lighten teachers' workloads, create transparency about student progress, increase a sense of personal responsibility for the work students submit, and encourage a conversation about the students' work and how they can continually improve. However, teachers need to lean on blended learning models to create the time and space for side-by-side grading.

As the class works on a task independently or with peer support, the teacher pulls one student at a time for their assessment. The goal is to create clarity around student performance. So, this is how it works.

1. Select a finished writing product or assessment (e.g., essay, research paper, scientific writing) to grade with students.
2. Be strategic about which writing elements to assess.
3. Use a writing-standards-aligned rubric to assess student work.
4. Set up a space in the classroom for these side-by-side writing assessments that provides a degree of privacy but also allows you to see the class.
5. Universally design a blended lesson or series of lessons that students can complete with little to no teacher guidance.
6. Identify a strategy to capture notes about student performance during these conversations so you can use that to design future differentiated lessons to meet specific student needs.
7. Think about the details. How much time will you spend with students? How will you quickly transition students in and out of the side-by-side assessments?

Strategy #1: Select a Finished Product or Assessment to Grade with Students

Teachers who attempt to grade everything students write will find this strategy unrealistic. Instead, it is important to be selective about which writing assignments will be graded and why. Because there are so many different ways to use writing in a classroom, teachers must ask the question "What is the purpose of this writing assignment?" when deciding which writing assignments to pull into a side-by-side assessment.

Students may complete quick writes or freewrites to share their thinking on a topic informally. They may respond to questions to demonstrate basic comprehension of concepts, issues, processes, or phenomena. They may write to make connections between key concepts in a text, video, podcast, or other resource. Writing may be a vehicle intended to deepen their understanding or make meaning as they learn about a subject. Writing may also be used to encourage a reflective process or to help to develop students' metacognitive muscles, helping them think about their learning in an intentional way. All of these are valuable uses for writing across the curriculum, which is part of the reason we take issue with the idea that writing is something that only happens in an English class. It should be happening in every class.

Yet, none of these are assessments intended to demonstrate mastery. If the purpose of the writing, be it a formal essay, lab report, scientific reasoning, research paper, or narrative, is to communicate effectively what was learned and to demonstrate mastery of specific skills, those are the pieces of writing that will benefit from the side-by-side assessment process.

Strategy #2: Be Strategic about Which Writing Elements to Assess

This is the first challenge many teachers encounter: they feel pressure to grade every aspect of every assignment every time. Why? If you are using a standards-aligned rubric that's been developed by your department or school district, it likely has many different criteria that cover every aspect of the type of writing assignment you are assessing. Teaching writing, however, happens in stages, with the more foundational aspects first (e.g., writing a claim or clear statement) and the more complex or nuanced elements of writing (e.g., reasoning, analysis, tone) developing over time.

Teachers should instead be strategic about what they assess at a particular moment in the school year. If a science teacher asks students to use scientific reasoning to explain a phenomenon, drawing on evidence and presenting clear reasoning, they may choose to assess one or two fundamental aspects of a student's writing at the start of the year, saving more sophisticated elements of the writing and reasoning process for later, when students have had more time to hone those skills.

To make side-by-side assessments sustainable for teachers and beneficial for students, it is best to identify two or three criteria to focus on during these conversations. That way, the conversations will not take so long that the strategy is unsustainable, and the amount of feedback students receive about their writing won't be overwhelming and hard to process.

Strategy #3: Use a Writing Standards-Aligned Rubric to Assess Student Work

Using a standards-aligned, mastery-based rubric keeps teachers focused during this assessment process and provides students with feedback on their writing. This may be a department- or district-approved rubric, a teacher-designed, standards-based rubric, or a student-designed rubric that reflects their understanding of the essential elements of this type of writing and what each element looks like at the different levels of mastery. Some teachers may be required to use a specific rubric, while others may be able to design their own. Regardless of the rubric teachers use, limiting the criteria assessed as suggested above will make this process run more smoothly for everyone.

Because teachers have likely dedicated significant time to the feedback process as students have written this piece (as discussed in chapter 6), side-by-side assessments are not the time to provide additional written feedback. Instead, as the teacher conducts a think-aloud, making their thinking about the student's writing explicit, they simply circle the language on the rubric that most closely aligns with what they see in the student's work. That way, students are receiving feedback in the form of a rubric, but teachers are not feeling pressured to write feedback on a finished product.

Let's look at the elementary narrative writing rubric pictured below (Figure 10.1). This rubric is aligned with the Common Core State Standards writing criteria. It uses a four-point mastery-based scale to describe what each element of writing looks like at each level of mastery. Although this is the most cognitively challenging aspect of creating a rubric like this, since teachers (or students) need to think about what writing looks like in the beginning, developing, proficient, and mastery stages, writing clear, student-friendly descriptions for each stage will save time and create clarity during side-by-side assessments. As teachers conduct their think-aloud simply circling language on the rubric to highlight strong or absent elements, or areas for further development, students can see their score for each element of the writing process as they are assessed.

Figure 10.1: Elementary Narrative Writing Rubric

Elementary Narrative Writing Rubric

Element	Beginning 2	Developing 2	Proficient 3	Mastery 4
Establishes Situation and Introduces Characters	Situation is unclear. Narrator is not introduced and characters are poorly developed.	Attempts to establish a situation. Introduces narrator and develops at least one character.	Establishes a situation, introduces the narrator, and develops characters.	Establishes a clear situation, introduces the narrator, and develops interesting characters.
Narrative Techniques	Little to no attempt to use dialogue, description, and pacing. Experiences and events are underdeveloped throughout.	Attempts to use dialogue, description, and pacing, however, experiences and events are underdeveloped.	Uses dialogue, description, and pacing to develop experiences and events.	Effectively uses dialogue, description, and pacing to develop experiences and events.
Sequence of Events	Unclear sequence of events. Plot is hard to follow throughout.	Attempts to sequence events. Plot is hard to follow in places.	Clear sequence of events that unfold naturally.	Clear, purposeful sequence of events that unfold naturally.
Conclusion	Abrupt ending. No clear resolution.	Ends with concluding statement that does not clearly follow from the narrative.	Ends with a clear resolution and concluding statement that follows from the narrative.	Effectively ends with a strong resolution and concluding statement that follows from the narrative.
Organization and Transitions	Little to no attempt at organization.	Attempts to organize ideas, but transitional language needs to be added.	Organizes ideas in a logical way. Transitional language used.	Strong organization and transitional language used throughout.
Mechanics (spelling and grammar)	Distracting mechanical errors throughout.	Mechanical errors distract at times.	A couple of errors present, but they do not distract.	Mechanics reflect careful editing.

At the beginning of the year, when students complete their first narrative writing assignment, the teacher may choose to focus their assessments on the criteria of "establishes situation and introduces characters" and "sequence of events," saving elements like "narrative techniques" and "mechanics" for later in the year, when they've dedicated more time to helping students develop and refine those skills. Again, it is critical to keep in mind that teachers do not need to grade every aspect of every writing assignment every time. Not only is it time-consuming, but we may be assessing aspects of the writing process that students have not had much practice with yet.

Strategy #4: Universally Design a Blended Lesson

During side-by-side writing assessments, teachers must work with one student at a time, so they cannot be actively engaged in the lesson the rest of the class is working on. Instead, they need to universally design a self-directed blended lesson, and students will need to use each other as resources if they get stuck or need support.

Depending on the grade level and subject area, teachers can choose from a collection of blended strategies and models that allow students to work independently, with a partner, or as part of a small group through a learning activity or sequence of activities. Table 10.1 presents some ideas for teachers to consider.

Table 10.1: Blended Learning Models and Strategies

Blended Learning Models and Strategies	
Choice Board	Teachers can present students with a choice board to work through, selecting a specific number of activities to complete in a lesson or series of lessons. • Standards-aligned choice board • Review-and-practice choice board • Thematic choice board
Self-paced Free-flow Station Rotation	Teachers can design a free-flow station rotation (without a teacher-led station) and allow students to self-pace through the online and offline learning activities, moving between stations as they finish tasks. They can integrate meaningful choices at each station with a "would you rather" option to remove barriers.
Three-part Flipped Lesson	Teachers can present a three-part, self-paced lesson built around video content. • Part 1: Access and share prior knowledge or complete a hook activity. • Part 2: Watch the video individually or with a partner, taking traditional notes or drawing sketchnotes. • Part 3: Individually or with a partner, practice and apply.
Playlist	Teachers can construct a playlist or sequence of learning activities, to move students toward a specific learning objective. It's a one-stop-shop, self-paced learning experience that includes all of the instruction, resources, and activities students need to direct their learning.

Strategy #5: Set up a Space for Side-by-Side Assessments

Before side-by-side assessments, teachers will want to select a space conducive to these conversations. We've found a student desk in the corner of the classroom is ideal, so teachers can quickly scan the room between assessment conversations to see if anyone needs help or is off task and needs redirection.

A high-top table, student desk, or side table is preferable to using the teacher's desk, which students may find intimidating. A high-top table gives the best view to monitor the room, but any desk or table that can accommodate two people will work.

Strategy #6: Identify a Strategy to Capture Notes about Student Performance

The purpose of side-by-side assessments is to measure student progress toward learning objectives and create transparency in the grading process. There isn't time to provide each student with personalized instruction during these assessment conversations. Instead, teachers should have a strategy to capture student questions that need to be addressed with additional instruction or models and to document which students need additional support and reteaching on a particular concept or skill.

We suggest teachers print out a sheet of paper with the criteria or elements of students' work being assessed at the top, as pictured in Figure 10.2. Then, as they meet with students, they can add names for those who would benefit from additional instruction and support in the corresponding column. Teachers can use this document when designing future lessons to provide specific students with differentiated or needs-based small-group instruction.

Figure 10.2: Document the Names of Students Who Need Follow-up Instruction and Support

Side-by-Side Assessment: Follow-up Instruction and Support		
Claim	Evidence	Explanation/Analysis
Questions:		

If teachers have a strategy to document who needs follow-up instruction and support, they are less likely to fall into the habit of trying to provide rushed instruction during these assessment conversations. That high-quality instruction demands time and can cause side-by-side assessments to take significantly longer, which may make this strategy feel unsustainable. Instead, let students know you will follow up on specific aspects of the assignment they struggled with in small-group sessions. This can alleviate the pressure to rush instruction during side-by-side assessments while reassuring students who are struggling that they will receive the support they need to continue progressing toward standards-aligned goals.

After they've conducted the think-aloud and circled language on the rubric, we encourage teachers to ask each student if they have any questions. Often the answer is no because students have received feedback throughout the process of writing. However, if they do have a question, the teacher can either choose to answer it or add it to a list of questions to address with the entire class.

Strategy #7: Details, Details, Details!

As with most new instructional strategies, the details can often trip a teacher up the first few times they try something. Teachers should consider the following:

- Figure out how much time you will have with each student, and set a timer to keep yourself on track.
- Decide how you will quickly transition students into and out of these side-by-side assessments.
- Make paper copies of your rubric, so you can fill them out as you conduct your think-aloud.

Teachers who think about and prepare for these aspects of side-by-side assessments will find the process runs smoother and more efficiently.

AI-Enhanced Strategy: Automated Assessment with AI Technology

There are numerous amazing solutions that provide students with instant feedback on spelling and grammar while also offering tips on writing style and clarity. As students draft and revise their writing, you can encourage them to use one of these tools before a side-by-side assessment with you as a teacher. For example, when we were drafting this AI-enhanced strategy, Grammarly rated our level of engagement as a "bit bland," as we overused words like *writing* and *revision*. Getting personalized tips, like the one below, allowed us to increase engagement and readability before sharing with our editor.

> ~~writing~~ → paper   essay
>
> The word **writing** appears repeatedly in this text. Consider using a synonym in its place.

Additionally, there are various automated grading tools, such as Turnitin and Paperrater, that use artificial intelligence and machine-learning algorithms to grade assignments and provide feedback while also inspecting them for plagiarism. These tools can save teachers significant time and effort in grading. We shared the draft of this strategy with Paperrater and received the following feedback.

- Excellent job! There are no signs of plagiarism throughout your work.
- Your phrases need some work. You may wish to use a thesaurus to replace or reduce your usage of the following words and/or phrases in your paper: *writing, revision, amazing.*

Welp, at least AI was consistent!

Wrap-Up

Assessing student work to identify the level of mastery in relation to subject-area content knowledge and skills is a critical part of a teacher's job. However, traditional approaches can often lead to teachers grading in isolation at home and returning graded work to students who do not understand why they are receiving specific scores. Instead, we want teachers to use grading as a vehicle to connect with students and strengthen their relationships with learners. When we grade with and for students, we create opportunities for conversation around student work and progress. We demystify the grading process, so students understand where they are in their progress toward mastering specific concepts and skills. This understanding of themselves is critical if they are to develop into expert learners who know their strengths, limitations, and areas of need.

So, instead of dragging assessments home and grading them on your evenings and weekends, we hope you'll be strategic about what you grade and design learning experiences that allow students to drive their learning while you facilitate these powerful side-by-side assessments. Not only will students have a clearer understanding of their progress and their assessment scores, but you won't have to spend endless evenings and weekends grading. As a recap, the following strategies can help you get your time back!

- Strategy #1: Select a Finished Product or Assessment to Grade *with* Students
- Strategy #2: Be Strategic about Which Writing Elements to Assess
- Strategy #3: Use a Writing-Standards-Aligned Rubric to Assess Student Work
- Strategy #4: Universally Design a Blended Lesson
- Strategy #5: Set up a Space for Side-by-Side Assessments
- Strategy #6: Identify a Strategy to Capture Notes about Student Performance
- Strategy #7: Details, Details, Details!
- AI-Enhanced Strategy: Automated Assessment with AI Technology

Reflect/Discuss

1. What student writing do you currently grade?
2. Do you use rubrics to assess finished products? If so, do you make these rubrics available at the start of the student's work on a product that will be assessed?
3. How do you determine the criteria you use to assess student work? Is it standards-aligned? Do you include criteria that fall more into a compliance or general work habits category?
4. What would the value for you and your students be if you only assessed finished products and used class time to grade with students? What impact might that have on student motivation and the quality of work they submit?

5. What blended learning models (e.g., playlist) or strategies (e.g., choice boards) could you use to create the time and space needed to conduct side-by-side assessments?
6. What would you ask students to do following side-by-side assessments to increase impact and effectiveness (e.g., revisions, reflection)?

Putting It into Practice

Select a piece of writing for assessment and design a standards-aligned, mastery-based rubric identifying two or three criteria you want to assess.

On your own or with a colleague, spend time describing what each criterion looks like at each level of mastery. Determine how much time you'll ideally want with each student (for example, 3–5 minutes). Then decide what type of blended learning model or strategy you will use to create the time and space to conduct these conversations.

Once you have designed your lesson and have a rubric, share them with a colleague or your professional learning network for feedback.

CONCLUSION

Humans Are Winning

The Magic of Walmart Jeans

Katie Recently, I had the opportunity to present right outside of Austin, Texas. I was excited to collaborate with a group of elementary teachers at a school committed to UDL implementation. I had to take a late flight from Boston, so I didn't arrive at my hotel until 1:30 a.m. Plenty of time for a nap! I set my alarm for 5:30 a.m. because the principal of the school would be picking me up at my hotel at 6:30 a.m. What could go wrong?

When my alarm went off, I rolled out of bed and unpacked my bag, ready to lay out my clothes so I could iron them. Adorable black sweater with apples on it? Check! Red shoes to match the adorable apple sweater? Check! Black pants to pull the outfit together? Hmmm.

I started rifling through the bottom of the bag like it belonged to Mary Poppins. It soon became clear that the black pants hadn't made the cut into the carry-on, and the blue sweatpants I'd worn on the plane and slept in weren't my most professional look. Worry not—I am nothing if not a problem solver. Problem-solving, like writing, is a process. Deep breaths.

Shift Writing into the Classroom

I took a minute and engaged in a pre-thinking activity. I had options, right? I brainstormed three of them: 1) sift through the hotel lost and found, 2) call the principal and ask if he knew someone about my size who wouldn't mind sharing, and 3) find a twenty-four-hour store that was selling pants at 5:30 a.m. A quick Google search identified numerous Walmarts in the area that were open at 6:00 a.m.

I started to plan. I showered and put on makeup in record time, threw on my sweats and sparkling red shoes, and waited by the curb for my Uber, sending a quick text to the principal to pick me up at Walmart because I'd forgotten a few necessities. Bless his heart, he responded, "That is an entry in a chapter for sure!!!! There are several Walmarts around—if you would pin me which one you are at, I'll be happy to get you from there!" (Thanks, Matt!) I greeted the opening crew at Walmart at 6:00 a.m., grabbed a pair of jeans, and was ready for the day. The jeans fit like a glove and were less than twelve dollars. Expert learning for the win, for sure!

Now, here's the thing. I didn't get my outfit right the first time, but I was able to reflect and come up with a new plan, and it gave me a great story to start the day. Now, why tell this story to end a book about writing? First, although my journey was possible *because* of technology, without goal setting, critical thinking, and some collaboration with Matt, it wouldn't have worked. We have to recognize that technology is a tool, and one that can make our lives so much easier. My phone, Google, Maps, Uber, and texting made a bit of a funny dilemma into a great story. One that I wrote myself and that ChatGPT could never come close to drafting. It is *my* story. Not the robot's. And I'm proud of it.

Throughout this book, Cat and I have shared the power and the promise of shifting writing instruction into classrooms in ways that are student-led. We want students to understand the purpose of writing, to find and share their voice, and to recognize that the best writing utilizes a process, numerous tools, and collaboration with peers and teachers. We shouldn't fear the chatbots in these classrooms because they are nothing more than a tool students can use to make their own writing process more efficient and more effective.

Research and Reality

Just as quickly as ChatGPT was released, there were countermeasures in education to address it. No surprise to us, the shifts align with best practices in UDL and blended learning. Within days of its release, there were news stories about schools and colleges adapting how they design and deliver instruction. A *New York Times* article, "Alarmed by A.I. Chatbots, Universities Start Revamping How They Teach," shared the following anecdote from a philosophy professor at Northern Michigan University[5]:

> Alarmed by [the discovery of ChatGPT], [the instructor] decided to transform essay writing for his courses this semester. He plans to require students to write first drafts in the classroom, using browsers that monitor and restrict computer activity. In later drafts, students have to explain each revision. Mr. Aumann, who may forgo essays in subsequent semesters, also plans to weave ChatGPT into lessons by asking students to evaluate the chatbot's responses.

We celebrate news like the example above, as we have long advocated for shifting to more in-class writing instruction, focusing on revisions, and empowering students to critically analyze exemplars. These practices empower students to learn more about the writing process, reflect on revisions, and develop the nuances of their own writing voice.

Generative AI will also require educators to think differently about the discipline-specific writing prompts we provide. The article goes on to say, "Gone are prompts like 'write five pages about this or that.' Some professors are instead crafting questions they hope will be too clever for chatbots and asking students to write about their own lives and current events."

What we know for sure is that tech tools like ChatGPT aren't going away.[6] OpenAI is expected to release another tool that's better at generating text than previous versions. Microsoft is discussing a $10 billion investment in OpenAI, while Google has built LaMDA, a rival chatbot that powers Bard. And with the chatbots came the chatbox disruptors. For example, Princeton senior Edward Tian made news because his app, GPTZero, can root out text composed by AI bots with a false positive rate of less than 2 percent. An article from NPR shares more about Tian's solution[7]:

> To determine whether an excerpt is written by a bot, GPTZero uses two indicators: "perplexity" and "burstiness." Perplexity measures the complexity of text; if GPTZero is perplexed by the text, then it has a high complexity and it's more likely to be human-written. However, if the text is more familiar to the bot—because it's been trained on such data—then it will have low complexity and therefore is more likely to be AI-generated. Separately, burstiness compares the variations of sentences. Humans tend to write with greater burstiness, for example, with some longer or complex sentences alongside shorter ones. AI sentences tend to be more uniform. In a demonstration video, Tian compared the app's analysis of a story in the *New Yorker* and a LinkedIn post written by ChatGPT. It successfully distinguished writing by a human versus AI. Tian acknowledged that his bot isn't foolproof, as some users have reported when putting it to the test. He said he's still working to improve the model's accuracy. But by designing an app that sheds some light on what separates human from AI, the tool helps work toward a core mission for Tian: bringing transparency to AI.

Instead of riding the waves of the artificial intelligence wars, we want to focus on classroom instruction that works in light of these advances. When we leverage Universal Design for Learning (UDL) and blended learning in our classrooms, we honor students as capable of thinking, planning, writing, revising, and sharing brilliant, authentic, and original work within and beyond the classroom community. To ensure that students have access to these experiences, we have to shift our teaching practices so that we can guide our students as they hone their voices and learn to communicate effectively based on task, purpose, and audience.

We could have used a chatbot to write this book, but you wouldn't hear our voices. Instead, you would have a technically well-written text that is mostly accurate and largely stale. We believe in the power of teachers and teaching, and we believe in kids. Although you may be able to ask ChatGPT to generate a response, it cannot execute a plan. Only humans can do that. Don't believe us? We want to get the last word, but before we do, let's ask ChatGPT what it would do if it forgot to pack its pants.

> Katie and Cat: I am on a business trip, and I forgot to pack my pants. It is 5:30 a.m. What should I do?
>
> ChatGPT: You have several options:
>
> 1. Wear alternative clothing: If you have alternative clothing such as shorts or a skirt, you can wear that until you have the opportunity to purchase new pants.
> 2. Utilize hotel services: If your hotel offers a 24-hour front desk, they may have a solution or suggestion for you, such as a lending program for forgotten items or directing you to a nearby 24-hour convenience store.
>
> Katie and Cat: We don't have alternative clothing, and a convenience store will not have professional clothes.

In a last-ditch effort, ChatGPT came to the rescue with this nugget.

> If you can't purchase new pants or wear alternative clothing, and it's still 5:00 a.m., you can consider the following option. Contact your hotel's front desk and inquire about their lending program or if they can provide a temporary solution, such as a loaner pair of pants or a robe.

Oh. My. Word. We can't even handle this one. In closing, if you ever see us in a professional setting wearing a hotel robe, please, we beg you, just loan us some pants.

Humans are winning. That is all.

Reflect/Discuss

1. What are the most significant barriers to incorporating student-led writing in your content area? How will this book help to address those barriers?
2. After reading the book, what is an essential idea that stuck with you that you want to incorporate into your writing instruction right away?
3. How will your writing instruction transform as a result of reading this text? Consider writing a response to post on social media, or record audio or video to share with your colleagues or the two of us!

Notes

Introduction
1. Education Week. "The Science of Reading . . . and Writing," January 17, 2023. https://www.edweek.org/teaching-learning/the-science-of-reading-and-writing.

Chapter 1
1. Anne Meyer, David Gordon, and David H. Rose, *Universal Design for Learning: Theory and Practice* (Wakefield, MA: CAST Professional Publishing, 2014).

Chapter 2
1. Katie Novak, *UDL Now! A Teacher's Guide to Applying Universal Design for Learning in Today's Classrooms*, 3rd ed. (Wakefield, MA: CAST Professional Publishing, 2022).
2. Troy Hicks, "What Research Says about Driving Growth for Writers With Practice, Feedback and Revision," *EdSurge*, November 6, 2017. https://www.edsurge.com/news/2017-11-06-what-research-says-about-driving-growth-for-writers-with-practice-feedback-and-revision.
3. Susan H. McLeod and Margot Soven (eds.), *Writing across the Curriculum: A Guide to Developing Programs*. The WAC Clearinghouse, 2000.
4. National Institute for Literacy. "What Content-Area Teachers Should Know about Adolescent Literacy." 2007. https://lincs.ed.gov/publications/pdf/adolescent_literacy07.pdf.
5. Steve Graham, Sharlene A. Kiuhara, and Meade MacKay, "The Effects of Writing on Learning in Science, Social Studies, and Mathematics: A Meta-Analysis," *Review of Educational Research* 90, no. 2 (March 19, 2020): 179–226. https://doi.org/10.3102/0034654320914744.
6. Fatih Kayaalp, Elif Meral, and Zeynep Başci Namli, "An Analysis of the Effect of Writing-to-Learn Activities Regarding Students' Academic Achievement and Self-Regulation Skills in Writing," *Participatory Educational Research* 9, no. 1 (January 1, 2022): 324–48. https://doi.org/10.17275/per.22.18.9.1.
7. Mustapha Chmarkh, "'Writing to Learn' Research: A Synthesis of Empirical Studies (2004–2019)," *European Journal of Educational Research* 10, no. 1 (January 15, 2021): 85–96. https://doi.org/10.12973/eu-jer.10.1.85.
8. Ibid.
9. McLeod and Soven, *Writing across the Curriculum*.
10. International Literacy Association, "Literacy Leadership Brief: Content Area and Disciplinary Literacy: Strategies and Frameworks." 2017. https://www.literacyworldwide.org/docs/default-source/where-we-stand/ila-content-area-disciplinary-literacy-strategies-frameworks.pdf.
11. ReLeah Lent, "Disciplinary Literacy: A Shift That Makes Sense," *EL* 12, no. 12 (2017). https://www.ascd.org/el/articles/disciplinary-literacy-a-shift-that-makes-sense.

12 "Writing-to-Learn Activities," The WAC Clearinghouse, accessed January 3, 2023, https://wac.colostate.edu/repository/resources/teaching/intro/wtl/wtlactivities/.
13 "Teaching Secondary Students to Write Effectively," What Works Clearinghouse (WWC), accessed January 3, 2023, https://ies.ed.gov/ncee/wwc/practiceguide/22.
14 Jennifer Gonzalez, "7 Easy Ways to Support Student Writing in Any Content Area." Cult of Pedagogy, 2015. https://www.cultofpedagogy.com/content-area-literacy-writing/.
15 "Teaching Secondary Students to Write Effectively," What Works Clearinghouse (WWC).

Chapter 3

1 Margaret R. Kirkland and Mary Anne P. Saunders, "Maximizing Student Performance in Summary Writing: Managing Cognitive Load," *TESOL Quarterly* 25, no. 1 (1991): 105–121.
2 "The Nation's Report Card: Writing 2011: Executive Summary," National Center for Education Statistics, accessed January 23, 2023, https://nces.ed.gov/nationsreportcard/pubs/main2011/2012470.aspx.
3 National Commission on Writing, "The Neglected 'R': The Need for a Writing Revolution," 2003. https://archive.nwp.org/cs/public/print/resource/2523.
4 Steve Graham, "Changing How Writing Is Taught," *Review of Research in Education* 43, no. 1 (March 2019): 277–303. https://doi.org/10.3102/0091732X18821125.
5 Ibid.
6 Novak, *UDL Now!*
7 Sheri Stover, Sharon G. Heilmann, and Amelia Hubbard, "Learner-Centered Design: Is Sage on the Stage Obsolete?," *Journal of Effective Teaching in Higher Education* 1, no. 1 (November 3, 2018): 3.
8 Russ Quaglia, Kristine Fox, Lisa Lande, and Deborah Young, *The Power of Voice in Schools: Listening, Learning, and Leading Together* (Alexandria, VA: ASCD, 2020), 79.
9 "Teaching Secondary Students to Write Effectively," What Works Clearinghouse (WWC), accessed January 3, 2023, https://ies.ed.gov/ncee/wwc/practiceguide/22.
10 Evan Gough, David DeJong, Trent Grundmeyer, and Mark Baron, "K-12 Teacher Perceptions Regarding the Flipped Classroom Model for Teaching and Learning," *Journal of Educational Technology Systems* 45, no. 3 (2017): 390–423.
11 Michael Carmichael, Abigail-Kate Reid, and Jeffrey D. Karpicke, "Assessing the Impact of Educational Video on Student Engagement, Critical Thinking and Learning." A SAGE white paper (2018). https://us.sagepub.com/sites/default/files/hevideolearning.pdf.
12 Philip J. Guo, Juho Kim, and Rob Rubin, "How Video Production Affects Student Engagement: An Empirical Study of MOOC videos," in *Proceedings of the First ACM Conference on Learning@Scale Conference*, 2014, 41–50.

Notes

Chapter 4

1. D. Royce Sadler, "Formative Assessment and the Design of Instructional Systems," *Instructional Science* 18, no. 2 (June 1989): 119–44. https://doi.org/10.1007/bf00117714.
2. Sheila R. Alber-Morgan, Terri Hessler, and Moira Konrad, "Teaching Writing for Keeps," *Education and Treatment of Children* 30, no. 3 (2007): 107–28. http://www.jstor.org/stable/42899937.
3. EL Education, "Austin's Butterfly: Building Excellence in Student Work," Vimeo video, 6:31. Friday, March 9, 2012, https://vimeo.com/38247060?embedded=true&source=vimeo_logo&owner=2957133.
4. Jennifer Gonzalez, "Dogfooding: How Often Do You Do Your Own Assignments?" Cult of Pedagogy, 2015. https://www.cultofpedagogy.com/dogfooding/.
5. "Teaching Secondary Students to Write Effectively," What Works Clearinghouse (WWC), accessed January 3, 2023, https://ies.ed.gov/ncee/wwc/practiceguide/22.
6. Literacy Design Collaborative, "LDC Task Templates for Grades 6–12," 2014. https://www.ccsoh.us/cms/lib/OH01913306/Centricity/Domain/207/LDC%20Task%20Templates%20for%20Grades%206%2012.pdf.
7. Literacy Design Collaborative, "LDC Task Templates for Grades 6–12," 2014. https://www.ccsoh.us/cms/lib/OH01913306/Centricity/Domain/207/LDC%20Task%20Templates%20for%20Grades%206%2012.pdf.
8. MSU Denver, "Teaching by Example and Nonexample," November 2, 2022. https://www.msudenver.edu/early-bird/teaching-by-example-and-nonexample/.
9. Heidi L. Andrade, Ying Du, and Xiaolei Wang, "Putting Rubrics to the Test: The Effect of a Model, Criteria Generation, and Rubric-Referenced Self-Assessment on Elementary School Students' Writing," *Educational Measurement: Issues and Practice* 27, no. 2 (2008): 3–13.

Chapter 5

1. Nejla Gezmiş, "Difficulties Faced by the Undergraduate Students in the Process Writing Approach," *Journal of Language and Linguistic Studies*, 16, no. 2 (June 28, 2020). https://doi.org/10.17263/jlls.759249.
2. Steve Graham, "Changing How Writing Is Taught," *Review of Research in Education* 43, no. 1 (March 2019): 277–303. https://doi.org/10.3102/0091732X18821125.
3. Bui Phu Hung and Le Thi Van, "Depicting and Outlining as Pre-Writing Strategies: Experimental Results and Learners' Opinions," *International Journal of Instruction* 11, no. 2 (April 3, 2018): 451–464.
4. Ibid.
5. Vararin Charoenchaikorn, "Prewriting in Voice Chat: Exploring the Effects of Collaborative Prewriting on EFL Learners' Performance," *Reflections* 29, no. 2 (May-August 2022): 278–300.
6. Ratnawati Mohd Asraf, Sabreena Ahmed, and Tan Kok Eng, "Using Focused Freewriting to Stimulate Ideas and Foster Critical Thinking during Prewriting," *TESOL International Journal* 13, no. 4 (2018): 67–81.

7. Anya S. Evmenova and Kelley Regan, "Supporting the Writing Process with Technology for Students with Disabilities," *Intervention in School and Clinic* 55, no. 2 (May 8, 2019): 78–85. https://doi.org/10.1177/1053451219837636.
8. Zeinab Shekarabi, "The Impacts of Outlining and Free Writing Strategies on the Quality of Japanese L2 Academic Writing Hiroshima University," *International Journal of Multidisciplinary Perspectives in Higher Education* 2 (2017): 63–76.
9. Purdue OWL. "How to Outline: Why and How to Create a Useful Outline," accessed 2023, https://owl.purdue.edu/owl/general_writing/the_writing_process/developing_an_outline/how_to_outline.html.
10. Patricia Hilliard, "Literacy Skills in Career and Technical Education Classes," *George Lucas Educational Foundation*, November 23, 2016. https://www.edutopia.org/article/literacy-skills-in-cte-classrooms-patricia-hilliard/.
11. Derek Martel (automotive instructor) in discussion with the author, January 2023.
12. Amy Rouse Gillespie and Steve Graham, "A Meta-Analysis of Writing Interventions for Students With Learning Disabilities," *Exceptional Children* 80, no. 4 (2014): 454–473. https://doi.org/10.1177/0014402914527238.

Chapter 6

1. John Hattie, *Visible Learning: A Synthesis of Over 800 Meta-Analyses Relating to Achievement* (New York: Routledge, 2008).
2. Robert J. Marzano, Debra Pickering, and Jane E. Pollock, *Classroom Instruction That Works: Research-Based Strategies for Increasing Student Achievement* (Alexandria, VA: ASCD, 2001).
3. Valerie J. Shute, "Focus on Formative Feedback," *ETS Research Report Series* 78, no. 1 (June 2007): i–47. https://doi.org/10.3102/0034654307313795.
4. Grant Wiggins, "Seven Keys to Effective Feedback," *Educational Leadership* 70, no. 1 (2012): 10–16.
5. David Boud and Elizabeth Molloy, "Rethinking Models of Feedback for Learning: The Challenge of Design," *Assessment and Evaluation in Higher Education* 38, no. 6 (September 2013): 698–712.
6. Hamideh Iraj, Anthea Fudge, Huda Khan, Margaret Faulkner, Abelardo Pardo, and Vitomir Kovanovic, "Narrowing the Feedback Gap: Examining Student Engagement with Personalized and Actionable Feedback Messages," *Journal of Learning Analytics* 8, no. 3 (2021): 101–116.
7. Stanford Teaching Commons, "Formative Assessment and Feedback." (n.d.) https://teachingcommons.stanford.edu/teaching-guides/foundations-course-design/feedback-and-assessment/formative-assessment-and-feedback.
8. Dai Hounsell, Velda McCune, Jenny Hounsell, and Judith Litjens, "The Quality of Guidance and Feedback to Students." *Higher Education Research and Development* 27, no. 1 (March 2008): 55–67.
9. Benedikt Wisniewski, Klaus Zierer, and John Hattie, "The Power of Feedback Revisited: A Meta-Analysis of Educational Feedback Research," *Frontiers in Psychology* 10 (2020): 3087.
10. Susanne Voelkel and Luciane V. Mello, "Audio Feedback—Better Feedback?" *Bioscience Education* 22, no. 1 (July 2014): 16–30.

11 Michael Henderson and Michael Phillips, "Video-Based Feedback on Student Assessment: Scarily Personal." *Australasian Journal of Educational Technology* 31, no. 1 (February 12, 2015).

Chapter 7

1 Aysegul Bayraktar, "Teaching Writing through Teacher-Student Writing Conferences," *Procedia-Social and Behavioral Sciences* 51 (2012): 709–713.
2 Elena Shvidko, "Writing Conference Feedback as Moment-to-Moment Affiliative Relationship Building," *Journal of Pragmatics* 127 (2018): 20–35.
3 Luxin Yang, "Focus and Interaction in Writing Conferences for EFL Writers." *SAGE Open* 12, no. 1 (2022). https://doi.org/10.1177/215824402110582.
4 Jay McTighe and Patrick L. Brown, "Using Understanding by Design to Make the Standards Come Alive," *Science Scope* 45, no. 2 (2021): 40–49.

Chapter 8

1 Kwangsu Cho and Charles MacArthur, "Student Revision with Peer and Expert Reviewing." *Learning and Instruction* 20, no. 4 (August 2010): 328–38.
2 Ibid.
3 Kirsten Jamson, "Making Peer Review Work." Writing Across the Curriculum. University of Wisconsin-Madison, 2017. https://dept.writing.wisc.edu/wac/making-peer-review-work/.
4 Colleen J. Soares, "Peer Review Methods for ESL Writing Improvement." Paper Presented at the Annual Meeting of the Teachers of English to Speakers of Other Languages, Seattle, Washington, March 17–21, 1998.
5 Jamson, "Making Peer Review Work."

Chapter 9

1 Amy Siegesmund, "Using Self-Assessment to Develop Metacognition and Self-Regulated Learners," *FEMS Microbiology Letters* 364, no. 11 (2017).
2 Ellen Schendel and Peggy O'Neill, "Exploring the Theories and Consequences of Self-Assessment through Ethical Inquiry." *Assessing Writing* 6, no. 2 (January 1999): 199–227.
3 Afsheen Rezai, Ehsan Namaziandost, and Siamak Rahimi, "Developmental Potential of Self-Assessment Reports for High School Students' Writing Skills: A Qualitative Study," *Teaching English as a Second Language Quarterly* (formerly *Journal of Teaching Language Skills*) 41, no. 2 (2022): 163–203.
4 Ibid.
5 Lois R. Harris and Gavin T. L. Brown, "Opportunities and Obstacles to Consider When Using Peer- and Self-Assessment to Improve Student Learning: Case Studies into Teachers' Implementation." *Teaching and Teacher Education* 36 (2013): 101–111.
6 Gary Bingham, Teri Holbrook, and Laura E. Meyers, "Using Self-Assessments in Elementary Classrooms." *Phi Delta Kappan* 91, no. 5 (2010): 59–61.
7 Heidi L. Andrade, Ying Du, and Xiaolei Wang, "Putting Rubrics to the Test: The Effect of a Model, Criteria Generation, and Rubric-Referenced Self-Assessment

on Elementary School Students' Writing," *Educational Measurement: Issues and Practice* 27, no. 2 (2008): 3–13.

8   Ernesto Panadero, Jesús Alonso Tapia, and Juan Antonio Huertas, "Rubrics and Self-Assessment Scripts Effects on Self-Regulation, Learning and Self-Efficacy in Secondary Education," *Learning and individual Differences* 22, no. 6 (2012): 806–813.

9   California Common Core State Standards: Mathematics. California State Board of Education. (2013)

Chapter 10

1   Daniel H. Pink, *Drive: The Surprising Truth about What Motivates Us* (New York: Penguin, 2011).

2   David M. Quinn, "Experimental Evidence on Teachers' Racial Bias in Student Evaluation: The Role of Grading Scales," *Educational Evaluation and Policy Analysis* 42, no. 3 (2020): 375–392.

3   Ken O'Connor, *How to Grade for Learning: Linking Grades to Standards* (Thousand Oaks, CA: Corwin, 2017).

4   Carol S. Dweck and David S. Yeager, "Mindsets: A View from Two Eras," *Perspectives on Psychological Science* 14, no. 3 (2019): 481–496.

5   Kalley Huang, "Alarmed by A.I. Chatbots, Universities Start Revamping How They Teach," *The New York Times*, January 16, 2023. https://www.nytimes.com/2023/01/16/technology/chatgpt-artificial-intelligence-universities.

6   Ibid.

7   Emma Bowman, "A College Student Created an App That Can Tell Whether AI Wrote an Essay," *NPR*, January 9, 2023. https://www.npr.org/2023/01/09/1147549845/gptzero-ai-chatgpt-edward-tian-plagiarism.

Acknowledgments

Catlin Katie: You are my absolute favorite writing partner! Thank you for embarking on yet another writing adventure with me. I am so grateful that our collaborations have brought us the incredible opportunity to meet and work together in person. Our time in Panama was amazing! I enjoyed starting each morning with a workout, working side-by-side to help educators shift to student-led workflows, delivering a two-person keynote, and winding down each evening over a meal and glass of wine!

Our work together has fueled my creativity and passion for this work. I hope the years ahead present us with many more opportunities to collaborate. I know I am a better writer and educator because of our work together. Thank you for being a remarkable collaborator and a kind and generous friend. Here's to the exciting journeys that lie ahead and the positive impact we will make together!

Cheyenne and Maddox: What can I say that I haven't said a million times? I love you more than life itself. You inspire and challenge me every day. I'm so proud of the kind, compassionate, curious, and capable humans you have become. I feel grateful every day for you and our relationship.

Christopher: You fill my life with laughter and love. I wake up every day grateful to have a partner who supports me and my work. You're the best sounding board, and your creative brain inspires me. Thank you for helping me achieve a healthier work-life balance with your gift for "shutting it down." I love ending the day on the porch with you talking.

George and Paige: Thank you for supporting our work! I appreciate all that you do to make these books a reality.

Katie

Cat: Oh my word, how I LOVE working with you. Honestly, we need to plan a yearly writing retreat that involves a tropical location of some kind. Obviously, while we travel, we will eat, drink, be merry, and send George some amazing GIFs of our hilarity. Truly, it is an honor to collaborate and learn from such an amazing and brilliant educator, writer, and momma. Cheers to many more years of friendship, more books, and hopefully, vacations that involve sun and sand.

My babies: Torin, Aylin, Brecan, and Boden. I am so damn blessed to be your momma. In this past year alone, we have made incredible memories that have included the engine crash in Kezar Lake, Winter Park, Colorado, the great upset at Trivia Night (Brec for the win!), and countless rounds of the Voting Game. Thank you for all choosing me as your one call if you get arrested. 😉 Remember to find joy in every moment, spread kindness, and please, stop arguing during basketball games. You have my whole heart, now and always.

Lon: As I write this, I can't help but remember we thought we were so clever when we got married, and we had our rings engraved with *There is only one*. That seemed super romantic until Jody burst out laughing during the rehearsal because she thought it was a *Lord of the Rings* allusion. Just know I would pick you over Frodo every time, as you have been my only one for twenty years, and it gets better every day. Oh, and just a written reminder, a Salt and Light honey cinnamon iced latte from the bank always brings a smile. xoxox

Acknowledgments

George: You're the older brother I never had, and every conversation convinces me that we're somehow related. Here's to countless belly laughs, a never-ending text chain filled with ridiculous memes, and many marathons in our future. Thank you for always believing in me. To Ashley, Paige, and Lindsey: Your dedication to keeping Cat and me on schedule, along with your support throughout the process of revisions, marketing, and production, is truly appreciated. Writing a book takes a village, and we're incredibly fortunate to have this strong sisterhood of publication.

About the Authors

About Catlin Tucker

Dr. Catlin Tucker is an author, international trainer, and keynote speaker. She was named Teacher of the Year in 2010 in Sonoma County, where she taught for sixteen years. Catlin earned her BA in English from the University of California at Los Angeles, her single subject teaching credential and master's in education from the University of California at Santa Barbara,  and her doctorate in learning technologies from Pepperdine University. Currently, Catlin is working as a blended learning coach, education consultant, and professor in the Master of Arts in Teaching program at Pepperdine University.

Catlin works with schools and districts all over the world, supporting their transition to blended learning. Catlin designs and facilitates professional learning to help leaders, coaches, and teachers to cultivate the mindset, skillset, and toolset necessary to thrive in any learning environment—in-person, online, or a blend of the two!

Catlin teaches educators how to blend the best aspects of online and offline learning to shift students to the center of learning. She also works with leadership teams and instructional coaches to explore how they can support the shift from teacher-led to student-led learning by developing a robust professional learning infrastructure that weaves professional learning into the fabric of the school.

Catlin has written a series of best-selling books on blended learning, which include *The Shift to Student-Led*, *The Complete Guide to Blended Learning*, *UDL and Blended Learning*, and *Balance with Blended Learning*. She is active on Twitter @Catlin_Tucker and Instagram @CatlinTucker and writes an internationally ranked blog at CatlinTucker.com.

About Katie Novak

Katie Novak, Ed.D., is an internationally renowned education consultant, author, graduate instructor at the University of Pennsylvania, and a former assistant superintendent of schools in Massachusetts. With twenty years of experience in teaching and administration, an earned doctorate in curriculum and teaching, and twelve published books, Katie designs and presents workshops both nationally and internationally, focusing on the implementation of inclusive practices, Universal Design for Learning (UDL), multi-tiered systems of support, and universally designed leadership. Novak's work has impacted educators worldwide, as her contributions and collaborations have built upon the foundation for an educational framework that is critical for student success.

Dr. Novak is the author of the best-selling books *UDL Now!: A Teacher's Guide to Applying Universal Design for Learning in Today's Classrooms*, *Innovate Inside the Box*, with George Couros, *Equity by*

Design, with Mirko Chardin, and *UDL and Blended Learning* and *The Shift to Student-Led* with Catlin Tucker.

Novak's work has been highlighted in many publications including *Edutopia, Cult of Pedagogy, Language, The Inclusion Lab* magazine, *NAESP Principal, ADDitude* magazine, *Commonwealth* magazine, the Huffington Post, *Principal Leadership, District Administrator, ASCD Education Update,* and *School Administrator.* You can learn more about Katie at novakeducation.com. She is also active on social media at @KatieNovakUDL.

More from

IMPRESS

ImpressBooks.org

Empower
What Happens when Students Own Their Learning
by A.J. Juliani and John Spencer

Learner-Centered Innovation
Spark Curiosity, Ignite Passion, and Unleash Genius
by Katie Martin

Unleash Talent
Bringing Out the Best in Yourself and the Learners You Serve
by Kara Knollmeyer

Reclaiming Our Calling
Hold On to the Heart, Mind, and Hope of Education
by Brad Gustafson

Take the L.E.A.P.
Ignite a Culture of Innovation
by Elisabeth Bostwick

Drawn to Teach
An Illustrated Guide to Transforming Your Teaching
written by Josh Stumpenhorst and illustrated by Trevor Guthke

Math Recess
Playful Learning in an Age of Disruption
by Sunil Singh and Dr. Christopher Brownell

Innovate inside the Box
Empowering Learners Through UDL and Innovator's Mindset
by George Couros and Katie Novak

Personal & Authentic
Designing Learning Experiences That Last a Lifetime
by Thomas C. Murray

Learner-Centered Leadership
A Blueprint for Transformational Change in Learning Communities
by Devin Vodicka

Kids These Days
A Game Plan for (Re)Connecting with Those We Teach, Lead, & Love
by Dr. Jody Carrington

UDL and Blended Learning
Thriving in Flexible Learning Landscapes
by Katie Novak and Catlin Tucker

Teachers These Days
Stories & Strategies for Reconnection
by Dr. Jody Carrington and Laurie McIntosh

Because of a Teacher
Stories of the Past to Inspire the Future of Education
written and curated by George Couros

Because of a Teacher, Volume 2
Stories from the First Years of Teaching
written and curated by George Couros

Evolving Education
Shifting to a Learner-Centered Paradigm
by Katie Martin

Adaptable
How to Create an Adaptable Curriculum and Flexible Learning Experiences That Work in Any Environment
by A.J. Juliani

Lead from Where You Are
Building Intention, Connection, and Direction in Our Schools
by Joe Sanfelippo

More from IMPress

The Shift to Student-Led
Reimagining Classroom Workflows with UDL and Blended Learning
by Catlin R. Tucker & Katie Novak

Evolving with Gratitude
Small Practices in Learning Communities That Make a Big Difference with Kids, Peers, and the World
by Lainie Rowell

The Design Thinking Classroom
Using Design Thinking to Reimagine the Role and Practice of Educators
by David Jakes

Be Great
Five Principles to Improve School Culture from the Inside Out
by Dwight Carter

Chasing Rabbits
A Curious Guide to a Lifetime of Mathematical Wellness
by Sunil Singh

Made in the USA
Thornton, CO
01/12/24 08:44:31

55304761-da91-4e33-9e39-93462010625cR01